AF480197

POCSO ACT- SUPREME COURT'S LATEST LEADING CASE LAWS

CASE NOTES- FACTS- FINDINGS OF APEX COURT JUDGES & CITATIONS

JAYPRAKASH BANSILAL SOMANI

Dedicated

To

All the Past & Present Judges of the Supreme Court of India.

Salute to their wisdom.

Salute to their interpretation of Law.

Salute to their elaborative judgement writing.

Contents

Contents

Preface

Dear Learned Advocates of the Trial Courts, Session Courts, High Courts, Supreme Court & Individuals,

I am very delighted to provide you a book on 'PROTECTION OF CHILDREN FROM SEXUAL OFFENCES ACT(POCSO)' - Supreme Court of India's Latest Leading Case Laws'.

In this book you will get...

1. Name of the Case i. e. Cause title

2.Relevant Sections discussed in the case

3. Hon'ble Judges/Coram of the case

4.Number of PDF Pages in Original Judgement of the case

5. All available Citations of the case

6. Case Note with appeal allowed/ dismissed or disposed off

7. Facts of the case

8. Hon'ble Apex Court's findings, while dismissing/allowing or disposing the appeal

9. Ratio Decidendi if any.

My special thanks to Manupatra, because of their web portal I can compile this book in well manner. I am also thankful to Notion Press to support me to publish & market this book throughout the Country. Thanks to my Juniors, Advocate Colleagues & Insolvency Professional Colleagues to support me in this venture.

Miss Aqsa Saharhas helped me a lot to compile this book.

I hope this book will add some value addition in the wealth of your legal knowledge. Your positive feedbacks will boost me to compile/ write further books & negative feedbacks will improve my skills. Kindly send your valuable feedbacks by email.

Thanks with Regards,

Jayprakash Bansilal Somani

Advocate, Supreme Court of India

Email: jaysomani64@gmail.com

Web Site:www.jayprakashsomani.com

Call: 9322188701, 8459194576

Acknowledgements

Printed & Published by
Notion Press
No. 8, 3rd Cross Street,
CIT Colony, Mylapore,
Chennai, Tamil Nadu- 600004
Managed by
Jayprakash Somani Advocates & Solicitors
Law Firm for Supreme Court of India
Delhi Office
B- 851, 1st Floor, Shivaji Marg, New Ashok Nagar, Delhi 110096.
Call: 9322188701, 8459194576
Supreme Court Chamber
312, 3rd Floor, M. C. Setalvad Block, In front of 'D' Gate, Bhagwan Das
Road, Supreme Court of India, New Delhi 110001
Contact: 8459194576, 9811011747
www.jayprakashsomani.com
Download our app to get access to our Free Videos, Free Bare Acts,
Free Study Material in Legal as well as International Business Regime.
Android App Link ;-https://clpandrea.page.link/cmSm
Ios APp Link :-https://apps.apple.com/us/app/classplus/id1324522260
Login with org code ;- (qywzji)
Web Link ;-https://qywzji.courses.store/
Opportunity for Lawyers/ Social Workers to get Supreme Court Law
Firm JSAS's authorised centre at District Level.
Kindly Message or Call to: 9322188701
Books are available online in India
1.**Notion Press:**https://notionpress.com/author/jayprakash_somani
2.**Amazon:**https://www.amazon.in/s?k=jayprakash+somani
3.**Flipkart:**https://www.flipkart.com/search?q=Jayprakash%20Somani
Books are available online at International Market
4. **Amazon International:** https://www.amazon.com/
s?k=jayprakash+somani
5. **Amazon United Kingdom:** https://www.amazon.co.uk/
s?k=jayprakash+somani

6. E-Books/Kindle edition at National & International Level:
https://www.amazon.in/s?k=jaypraksh+somani

CHAPTER ONE

Pappu Vs. The State of Uttar Pradesh, 2022

Hon'ble Judges/Coram:
A.M. Khanwilkar, Dinesh Maheshwari and C.T. Ravikumar, JJ.
Relevant Sections:
SECTIONS 498-A AND 304-B OF IPC, SECTION 113-B OF EVIDENCE ACT. Sections 376, 302, 201 of the Indian Penal Code, 1860 (IPC) and Section 5/6 of the Protection of Children from Sexual Offences Act, 2012
No. of pdf Pages of the Original Judgment: 46
Equivalent Citation:
2022(3)ADJ417, MANU/SC/0167/2022
Case Notes:
Criminal - Death sentence - Challenge thereto - Sections 376, 302, 201 of the Indian Penal Code, 1860 (IPC) and Section 5/6 of the Protection of Children from Sexual Offences Act, 2012 - Present appeals by special leave are directed against the judgment and order whereby, the High Court has affirmed the judgment and order as passed by the Additional Sessions Judge, and, while upholding the conviction of the Appellant of offences punishable under Sections 376, 302, 201 of the IPC and Section 5/6 of the Act, 2012, has confirmed the death sentence awarded to him for the offence under Section 302 of IPC - Whether death sentence be maintained or substituted by any other sentence?
Facts:

In present appeals, the conviction of the Appellant as also the punishment awarded to him, particularly the capital punishment, are under challenge. The Appellant has been Accused of enticing a seven-year-old girl to accompany him on the pretext of picking lychee fruits; having thereafter committed rape upon the child; having caused her death; and having dumped the dead body near a bridge on the riverbank, after having dragged the dead body over a distance of one and one-quarter kilometres.

Hon'ble Apex Court Held, while dismissing/ allowing the appeal:

i. It is proved beyond doubt in this case that the hapless child, seven-year-old daughter of the complainant, met with her gruesome end after having been treated inhumanely and having been subjected to sexual assaults; that the victim was lastly seen in the company of the Appellant when he enticed and took her along to pluck and eat lychee fruits while shooing away the other children playing with her; that the dead body of the victim child was recovered at the instance of the Appellant; and that the Appellant failed to satisfactorily explain his whereabouts and his knowledge of the location of dead body. The medical and other scientific evidence has been consistent with the prosecution case and then, the defence version of enmity due to land dispute turns out to be false. The Appellant was rightly convicted by the Trial Court and his conviction has rightly been maintained by the High Court.

ii. The impugned orders awarding and confirming death sentence could only be said to be of assumptive conclusions, where it has been assumed that death sentence has to be awarded because of the ghastly crime and its abhorrent nature. The tests and the norms laid down in the relevant decisions commencing from those in Bachan Singh v. State of Punjab seem not to have acquired the requisite attention of the Trial Court and the High Court. The approach of the Trial Court and the High Court in this matter while awarding sentence could only be disapproved.

iii. The heinous nature of crime like that of present one, in brutal rape and murder of a seven-year-old girl child, definitely discloses aggravating circumstances, particularly when the manner of its commission shows depravity and shocks the conscience. But, at the same time, it is noticeable that the Appellant has no criminal antecedents, comes from a very poor socio-economic background, has a family comprising of wife, children and aged father, and has unblemished jail conduct. When all these factors are added together and it is also visualised that there is nothing on record to Rule out the probability of reformation and rehabilitation of the Appellant, it would be unsafe to treat this case as falling in 'rarest of rare' category. Putting it differently, when the Appellant is not shown to be a person having criminal antecedents and is not a hardened criminal, it cannot be said that there is no probability of him being reformed and rehabilitated. His unblemished jail conduct and having a family of wife, children and aged father would also indicate towards the probability of his reformation.

iv. However, and even when the present case is taken to be not falling in the category of 'rarest of rare' so as to require termination of the life of the Appellant yet, the impact of the offences in question on the conscience of the society as a whole cannot be ignored. Thus, it appears just and proper to apply the course adopted in various cases involving the crimes of similar nature where, even while commuting capital punishment, this Court has provided for life imprisonment without application of the provisions of premature release/remission before mandatory actual imprisonment for a substantial length of time.

v. The Appellant was about 33-34 years of age at the time of commission of crime in the year 2015. Looking to the overall facts and circumstances, it would be just and proper to award the punishment of imprisonment for life to the Appellant for the offence under Section 302 of IPC while providing for actual imprisonment for a minimum period of 30 years. Having regard to the circumstances of this case and other punishments awarded to the Appellant, it is also just and proper to provide that all the substantive sentences shall run concurrently.

vi. The conviction of the Appellant of offences under Sections 376, 302, 201 of IPC and Section 5/6 POCSO is upheld and the sentences awarded to him are confirmed except the death sentence for the offence under Section 302 of IPC. The death sentence awarded to the Appellant for the offence under Section 302 of IPC is commuted into that of imprisonment for life, with the stipulation that the Appellant shall not be entitled to premature release or remission before undergoing actual imprisonment for a period of 30 (thirty) years. The other terms of sentences awarded to the Appellant, including the amount of fine and default stipulations, are also confirmed. The direction for payment of half of the amount of fine to the mother of the deceased girl is also confirmed. All the substantive sentences awarded to the Appellant shall run concurrently. Appeal partly allowed.

4

CHAPTER TWO

AHMAD ALI QURAISHI AND ORS. VS. THE STATE OF UTTAR PRADESH AND ORS., 2020

Hon'ble Judges/Coram:

Ashok Bhushan and M.R. Shah, JJ.

Relevant Sections:

Sections 482 Code of Criminal Procedure, 1973; Section 323, 353, 504, 506 of IPC and Section 7/8 POSCO Act.

No. of pdf Pages of the Original Judgment: 8

Equivalent Citation:

2020(214)AIC217, AIR2020SC788, 2020 (1) ALD(Crl.) 768 (SC), 2020(2) ALJ 691, 2020 (113) ACC 604, 2020 (2) ALT (Crl.) 388 (A.P.), 2020(1)Crimes134(SC), 2020(1)JLJ620, 2020(1)MLJ(Crl)662, 2020(3)RLW1813(SC), (2020)13SCC435, 2020(2)UC1085, MANU/SC/0104/2020

Case Notes:

Criminal - Quashing of proceedings - Section 482 Code of Criminal Procedure, 1973 (CrPC)- Present appeal had been filed challenging order of High Court by which application under Section 482 of CrPC filed by Appellants Accused to quash the proceedings of Complaint Case had been rejected - Whether criminal proceedings initiated by Complaint Case were liable to be quashed.

Facts:

The Appellants Accused and the Respondent No. 2 complainant belongs to same family and are neighbours. The father of the Accused Anwarul Haq has filed O.S. against the complainant in the court of Civil judge (Junior Division) with regard to partition of properties which suit is still pending. Suit between the parties led to several altercations among the parties. The Learned Sessions Judge by order summoned the Appellants under Section 323, 353, 504, 506 of IPC and Section 7/8 POSCO Act. The Appellant filed an application under Section 482 of CrPC in the High Court praying for quashing the entire proceeding of Complaint Case as well as the summoning order. The application has been dismissed by the High Court by the impugned judgment aggrieved against which judgment, this appeal has been filed.

Hon'ble Apex Court Held, while dismissing/ allowing the appeal:

i. The High Court in our considered opinion appear to have missed that assuming the trial court had This Court time and again has examined the scope of jurisdiction of the High Court Under Section 482 of CrPC and laid down several principles which govern the exercise of jurisdiction of the High Court under Section 482 of CrPC. A three-Judge Bench of this Court in State of Karnataka v. L. Muniswamy, held that the High Court is entitled to quash a proceeding if it comes to the conclusion that allowing the proceeding to continue would be an abuse of the process of the court or that the ends of justice require that the proceeding ought to be.

ii. It is clear that the present is a case where parties are related and are neighbours. Civil dispute regarding property is going on between father of the Accused and the complainant. The incident which is basis for summoning of Appellant is dated 19.07.2016 which is alleged to have taken place in front of the house of the complainant. The materials on record do indicate that quarrel took place between the parties on 19.07.2016 and police visited the spot and initiated proceedings under Section 151, 107 and 116 of CrPC.

iii. From the sequence of the events, it is clear that dispute regarding property between complainant and father of the Appellant is pending much before the alleged incident dated 19th July, 2016. The fact that on the same date of the incident Police visited the spot and has drawn proceeding under Section 151, 107, 116 of CrPC against both the parties and both the parties were required to maintain peace is a clear pointer to the nature of quarrel between the parties. It was more than six weeks thereafter that for the first time an application under Section 156(3) of CrPC was filed by the complainant against the Accused in the court of Session Judge.

iv. One more fact which transpire from order of Session Judge summoning the Accused need to be noted. The complaint against the Appellant and other Accused refers to two incidents of 19.07.2016. One incident which took place near the Public hand pump outside the house of complainant and second, on the same day in the house of the complainant where he alleged that the Appellants, their father and other Accused entered into the house and started beating the complainant and his daughters. Sessions Judge in his summoning order did not believe the second incident as alleged in the complaint. Non believing on one part of the incident as alleged in the complaint by the Court clearly throws a shadow of doubt on the earlier part of the incident as alleged.

v. Learned session judge in the impugned judgment has not taken note of the Civil Suit pending between the parties.

vi. Present is a case where criminal proceedings have been initiated by complainant with an ulterior motive due to private and personal grudge. The High Court although noticed the judgment of this Court in State of Haryana and Ors. v. Bhajan Lal and Ors. in the impugned judgment but did not examine the facts of the case as to whether present is a case which falls in any of the category as enumerated in Bhajan Lal's case. The present case clearly falls in category VII of Bhajan Lal's case and the High Court failed to exercise jurisdiction Under Section 482 of CrPC in quashing the criminal proceeding initiated by the complaint.

vii. In permitting Criminal proceedings against the Appellant shall be permitting a criminal proceeding which has been maliciously instituted with ulterior motives, permitting such criminal proceeding to go on is nothing but the abuse of the process of the Court which needs to be interfered by this Court.

viii. In result, the appeal is allowed. The criminal proceedings initiated by Complaint Case are quashed.

CHAPTER THREE

DATTATRAYA VS. THE STATE OF MAHARASHTRA, 2019

Hon'ble Judges/Coram:

N.V. Ramana, Deepak Gupta and Indira Banerjee, JJ.

Relevant Sections:

Sections 302, 376(2)(f), 377, 363, 364, 367 and 201 of Indian Penal Code, 1860; Sections 3, 4, 5(i) (l) and (m) of the Protection of Children from Sexual Offences Act, 2012

No. of pdf Pages of the Original Judgment: 25

Equivalent Citation:

2020(210)AIC137, AIR2019SC4589, 2020 (1) ALD(Crl.) 96 (SC), 2020ALLMR(Cri)36, 2020CriLJ215, 2019(4)JKJ385[SC], 2021(2)RCR(Criminal)1, 2019(13)SCALE187, (2020)14SCC290, MANU/SC/1001/2019

Case Notes:

Criminal - Conviction - Imposition of death sentence - Sections 302, 376(2)(f), 377, 363, 364, 367 and 201 of Indian Penal Code, 1860 (IPC) and Sections 3, 4, 5(i) (l) and (m) of the Protection of Children from Sexual Offences Act, 2012 (POCSO) - Present appeals were against final judgment of High Court whereby High Court had confirmed conviction of Appellant under Sections 302, 376(2)(f), 377, 363, 364, 367 and 201 of IPC, as also under Sections 3, 4, 5(i) (l) and (m) of POCSO and affirmed sentence of death imposed on Appellant - Whether impugned order of sentence was liable to be modified.

Facts:

Charges were framed against the Accused-Appellant under Sections 363, 364, 367, 377, 302, 201 and 376 or alternatively 376(2)(f) of the IPC. Charges were also framed Under Sections 3, 4 and 5 of POCSO. The Accused-Appellant pleaded not guilty and claimed to be tried. His defence was of denial and false implication. By a judgment, learned Special Judge (Protection of Children from Sexual Offences Act), convicted the Accused-Appellant of offences under Sections 363, 364, 367, 302, 201, 376, 376(2)(f) and 377 of IPC read with Sections 4 and 6 of POSCO. Accused-Appellant was produced in Court and heard on the question of sentence after which the Trial Court ordered that, Accused Dattatray @ Datta Ambo Rokde is hereby convicted of the offences punishable under Sections 363, 364, 367, 302, 201 of the IPC and under Sections 376, 376(2)(f), 377 of IPC r/w Section 3 punishable under Section 4 of the POSCO and under Sections 5(h)(i), 5(k), (l) (m) punishable under Section 6 of POSCO Act. Accused is sentenced to death for an offence punishable under Section 302 of the IPC and he be hanged by the neck till he is dead, subject to confirmation by Hon'ble High Court. Accused is sentenced to suffer imprisonment for life for offences under Sections 376, 376(2)(f), 377 of the IPC and offence under Section 3 punishable under Sections 4 and 5(h)(i), 5(k), (l) (m) punishable under Section 6 of the POSCO Act. No separate sentence is awarded for offences under Sections 363, 364, 367 and 201 of IPC. By a judgment, Division Bench of Bombay High Court confirmed the conviction and sentence of death imposed under Section 302 of the IPC on the Accused-Appellant. The appeal of the Accused-Appellant was partly allowed only to the extent that the conviction of the Accused-Appellant under Section 376 simplicitor was set aside. The State has not filed any appeal against the judgment and order of the Division Bench.

Hon'ble Apex Court Held, while dismissing/ allowing the appeal:

i. As argued on behalf of the Accused-Appellant, there may have been embellishment of the evidence against the Accused-Appellant. The evidence of the PWs 4 and 5 supported by PW-10 can never be the basis of any conviction and is fraught with inherent inconsistencies.

ii. Even assuming that PWs 4 and 5 actually noticed the Accused-Appellant carrying a bag and dumping it in the lane opposite the car shed, this was in the evening of 22.1.2013 whereas the body of the victim was first seen by her parents outside the door of their tenement, well past midnight, at around 2.00 a.m.

iii. Admittedly, these two witnesses had not noticed anything suspicious. A bag with the body of the child would, in all likelihood, have aroused suspicion. No other material was found to suggest that the body might have been concealed and/or wrapped and then put in the bag identified by PW-4 and PW-5. Admittedly, these two witnesses did not examine the bag carried by the Accused-Appellant (if at all) closely. No credence can be placed on identification by the PW 4 and 5, of the bag seized and produced by the Police, as the same bag carried by the Accused-Appellant. The identification is preposterous.

iv. It is equally true that none of the witnesses except PW-18, Asha, wife of the Accused-Appellant to whom the Accused-Appellant confessed his guilt and the PW-12, a Pancha, in whose presence the Accused-Appellant made extra judicial confession to the Police, is relevant to the guilt of the Accused-Appellant. However, it is reiterated at the cost of repetition that the forensic evidence supported by the evidence of PW-18 establishes the guilt of the Appellant beyond reasonable doubt. Conviction of the Accused-Appellant for the offences under Sections 302, 376(2)(f), 377 of the IPC read with Sections 3, 4 and 5 of the POCSO is confirmed.

v. Under the Indian Penal Code and, in particular, Section 299 thereof, whoever causes death by doing an act either with the intention of causing death or with the intention of causing such bodily injury as is likely to cause death or with the knowledge that he is likely, by such act, to cause death, commits the offence of culpable homicide..

vi. As per the definition of Section 300 of the Indian Penal Code, except in cases excepted thereafter, culpable homicide is murder if the act by which the death is caused (i) is done with the intention of causing death or (ii) if it is done with the intention of causing such bodily harm as the offender knows to be likely to cause the death of the person to whom the harm is caused or (iii) if the act is done with the intention of causing bodily injury to any person and the bodily injury intended to be inflicted is sufficient in the ordinary course of nature to cause death or (iv) if the person committing the act knows that it is so imminently dangerous that it must, in all probably, cause death or such bodily injury as is likely to cause death and commits such act without any excuse for incurring the risk of causing death or such injury as aforesaid.

vii. As a mature man, over fifty years of age, the Accused-Appellant should have known that the rape of a five year old child by an adult was dangerous and could lead to such injuries, as was in all probability likely to cause death.

viii. The death of the deceased victim was not caused under any provocation, not to speak of sudden provocation. No such defence has been taken by the Accused-Appellant. Nor is it anybody's case that the death was caused in legitimate exercise in good faith of any right of the Accused-Appellant, whether of private defence or otherwise. The death has been caused without any provocation.

ix. The totality of the injuries support the finding of the Trial Court and the First Appellate Court that the Accused-Appellant murdered the deceased victim. Though the act of the victim squarely amounts to rape and murder, there is not a scrap of material to show that the intention of the Accused-Appellant was to kill the minor child.

x. The PW-1, Dr. Bhusan Jain who had prepared the post mortem report opined that the cause of death was asphyxia due to smothering, associated with head injuries and sexual assault. Dr. Bhusan Jain deposed that all the 5 injuries were possible by repeated sexual acts and forceful penetration. He opined that all the injuries were sufficient to cause instant death in the ordinary course.

xi. Being a man of about 50 years of age, the Accused-Appellant should have known that repeated sexual assault could have led to the death of the victim and in fact did lead to the death of the victim, only five years of age. The Accused-Appellant has rightly been convicted of murder apart from child rape. However, there is no evidence at all direct or circumstantial which establishes that the intention of the Accused-Appellant was to kill the deceased victim.

xii. There can be no doubt that, rape and murder of a 5 years old girl shocks the conscience. It is barbaric. There is, however, no evidence to support the finding that the murder was pre-meditated. The Petitioner did not carry any weapon. The possibility that the Accused-Appellant might not have realized that his act could lead to death cannot altogether be ruled out. Moreover, the Trial Court has apparently not considered the question of whether the crime is the rarest of rare crimes as mandated by the Supreme Court in Bachan Singh.

xiii. The Accused-Appellant neither sought nor was given the opportunity to file any affidavit placing on record relevant mitigating circumstances. The legal assistance availed by the Accused-Appellant was patently not satisfactory and he was not accompanied by a social worker. No attempt was made to place on record mitigating circumstances. No argument was advanced to the effect that there was no similar case against the Accused-Appellant. In the absence of any arguments, the Trial Court did not consider the question of whether the Accused-Appellant could be reformed.

xiv. Considering the nature of the crime against a five year old child, the Trial Court imposed the extreme penalty of death without deciding the question of whether there was no alternative to imposing death sentence on the Accused-Appellant. There is no finding that in the absence of death sentence, the Accused-Appellant would continue to be a threat to the society. The question of whether the Accused-Appellant could be reformed, had not at all been considered.

xv. As held in Dagdu, irrespective of whether these issues were raised on behalf of the Accused, the Court is obliged on its own to elicit facts relevant to the question of existence of mitigating circumstances. The Court made no attempt to elicit any facts relevant to the sentence.

xvi. For effective hearing under Section 235(2) of the CrPC, the suggestion that the court intends to impose death penalty should specifically be made to the Accused, to enable the Accused to make an effective representation against death sentence, by placing mitigating circumstances before the Court. This has not been done. The Trial Court made no attempt to elicit relevant facts, nor did the Trial Court give any opportunity to the Petitioner to file an affidavit placing on record mitigating factors. As such the Petitioner has been denied an effective hearing.

xvii. Contrary to the dictum of this Court, in Dagdu and Santa Singh, Petitioner was not given a real, effective and meaningful hearing on the question of sentence Under Section 235(2) of the CrPC. The death sentence imposed on the Petitioner is liable to be commuted to life imprisonment on this ground.

xviii. There can be no doubt that the rape and murder of a five years old child is absolutely heinous and barbaric, but as observed above, it cannot be said to be in the category of rarest of rare cases.

xix. In Mulla and Anr. v. State of U.P., this Court has affirmed that it is open to the Court to prescribe the length of incarceration. This is especially true in cases where death sentence has been replaced by the life imprisonment. This Court observed, "the court should be free to determine the length of imprisonment which will suffice the offence committed."

xx. Even though life imprisonment means imprisonment for entire life, convicts are often granted reprieve and/or remission of sentence after imprisonment of not less than 14 years. In this case, considering the heinous, revolting, abhorrent and despicable nature of the crime committed by the Appellant, we feel that the Appellant should undergo imprisonment for life, till his natural death and no remission of sentence be granted to him.

xxi. Present appeals are one of such cases where we would be justified in holding that confinement till natural life of the Accused-Appellant shall fulfil the requisite criteria of punishment considering the peculiar facts and circumstances of the present case. Accordingly, the death sentence awarded by the trial court is hereby modified to "life imprisonment" i.e., imprisonment for the natural life of the Appellant. The appeals are allowed.

CHAPTER FOUR

ATTORNEY GENERAL FOR INDIA AND ORS. VS. SATISH AND ORS., 2021

Hon'ble Judges/Coram:
U.U. Lalit, Bela M. Trivedi and S. Ravindra Bhat, JJ.
Relevant Sections:
Sections 342, 354 and 363 of Indian Penal Code, 1860; Sections 7, 8 and 10 of the Protection of Children from Sexual Offences Act, 2012
No. of pdf Pages of the Original Judgment: 25
Equivalent Citation:
AIR2022SC13, 2022 (1) ALD(Crl.) 1 (SC), 2021ALLMR(Cri)4694, 2022(1)BLJ277, 2022CriLJ1, 2021(4)Crimes370(SC), 2022(1)J.L.J.R.257, 2022(1)JKJ289[SC], 2021(6)KLT604, 2022(1)PLJR211, 2022(1)RCR(Criminal)167, MANU/SC/1086/2021
Case Note:
Criminal - Aggravated sexual assault - Interpretation - Section 7 of the Protection of Children from Sexual Offences Act, 2012 (POCSO Act) -Trial Court convicted Accused for the offences under Sections 342, 354 and 363 of the IPC and Section 8 of the POCSO Act - High Court in appeal acquitted the Accused from Section 8 of the POCSO Act while maintaining conviction under Sections 342 and 354 of the IPC - Whether High Court while disposing appeals erred in interpreting Section 7 of the POSCO Act?
Facts:

In the case accusing Satish, informant (victim's mother) alleged Accused of taking her daughter to his house and committed sexual assault. Trial Court convicted the Accused for committing 'aggravated sexual assault'. High Court acquitted Accused for the offence under Section 8 of the POCSO Act and convicted him for the minor offence under Sections 342 and 354 of IPC by observing there was no direct physical contact i.e. skin to skin with sexual intent without penetration. In the other case where Libnus is accused, Trial Court convicted accused under Section 448 and 354-A(1)(i) of Indian Penal Code and Sections 8 and 10 read with Section 9(m) and 12 of the POCSO Act. High Court maintained the conviction under Sections 448 and 354-A(1)(i) of the IPC read with Section 12 of the POCSO Act and set aside the conviction under Sections 8 and 10 of POSCO Act. Hence the present appeals by State and also by Accused challenging conviction.

Hon'ble Apex Court Held, while dismissing/ allowing the appeal:

Bela M. Trivedi, J.

The act of touching any sexual part of the body of a child with sexual intent or any other act involving physical contact with sexual intent, could not be trivialized or held insignificant or peripheral so as to exclude such act from the purview of "sexual assault" Under Section 7.

The Court cannot be oblivious to the fact that the impact of traumatic sexual assault committed on children of tender age could endure during their whole life, and may also have an adverse effect on their mental state. The suffering of the victims in certain cases may be immeasurable. Therefore, considering the objects of the POCSO Act, its provisions, more particularly pertaining to the sexual assault, sexual harassment etc. have to be construed vis-a-vis the other provisions, so as to make the objects of the Act more meaningful and effective.

High Court fell into error in case of the Accused-Satish in holding him guilty for the minor offences under Sections 342 and 354 of Indian Penal Code and acquitting him for the offence under Section 8 of the POCSO Act. The High Court while specifically accepting the consistent versions of the victim and her mother i.e. informant about the Accused having taken the victim to his house, having pressed the breast of the victim, having attempted to remove her salwar and pressing her mouth, had committed gross error in holding that the act of pressing of breast of the child aged 12 years in absence of any specific details as to whether the top was removed or whether he inserted his hands inside the top and pressed her breast, would not fall in the definition of sexual assault, and would fall within the definition of offence under Section 354 of the Indian Penal Code. The High Court further erred in holding that there was no offence since there was no direct physical contact i.e. "skin to skin" with sexual intent.

The interpretation of Section 7 at the instance of the High Court on the premise of the principle of "ejusdem generis" is also thoroughly misconceived.

The prosecution had duly proved not only the sexual intent on the part of the Accused but had also proved the alleged acts that he had pressed the breast of the victim, attempted to remove her salwar and had also exercised force by pressing her mouth. All these acts were the acts of "sexual assault" as contemplated Under Section 7, punishable under Section 8 of the POCSO Act.

In the case other Accused-Libnus, High Court while recording the finding that the prosecution had established that the Accused had entered into the house of the prosecutrix with the intention to outrage her modesty, also held that the acts "holding the hands of the prosecutrix" or "opened the zip of the pant" did not fit in the definition of sexual assault. High Court had fallen into a grave error in recording such findings. When the alleged acts of entering the house of the prosecutrix with sexual intent to outrage her modesty, of holding her hands and opening the zip of his pant showing his penis, are held to be established by the prosecution, there was no reason for the High Court not to treat such acts as the acts of "sexual assault" within the meaning of Section 7 of the POCSO Act.

Impugned judgments quashed and set aside.

S. RavindraBhat, J.

The fallacyin High Court's reasoning is that it assumes that indirect touch is not covered by Section 7-or in other words is no "touch" at all. High Courtclearly erred in acting on such interpretation, and basing its conviction of and awarding sentence to the Respondents; as it did they were guilty of sexual assault. In the case of Satish, the conviction is to be under Section 8. In the case of Libnus, the appropriate conviction is of aggravated sexual assault, under Section 10. Appeals of the Accused dismissed.

CHAPTER FIVE

Eera through Manjula Krippendorf Vs. State (Govt. of NCT of Delhi) and Ors., 2017

Hon'ble Judges/Coram:

Rohinton Fali Nariman and Dipak Misra, JJ.

Relevant Sections:

Section 2(d) of Protection of Children from Sexual Offences Act, 2012 and Section 376(2)(1) of Indian Penal Code, 1860

No. of pdf Pages of the Original Judgment: 52

Equivalent Citation:

2018(182)AIC208, AIR2017SC3457, 2017 (2) ALD(Crl.) 673 (SC), 2018 (102) ACC 668, 2017(3)BomCR(Cri)593, 2018CriLJ186, 2018(2)Crimes99(SC), 2017(165)DRJ233, 2017(4)J.L.J.R.75, 2017(3)KLT560, 2017(3)MLJ(Crl)452, 2017(3)N.C.C.711, 2017(3)N.C.C.761, 2017(4)PLJR91, 2017(3)RCR(Criminal)734, 2017(8)SCALE112, (2017)15SCC133, 2019 (1) SCJ 662, MANU/SC/0876/2017

Case Notes:

Criminal - Determination of age - Application of Act - Section 2(d) of Protection of Children from Sexual Offences Act, 2012 and Section 376(2)(1) of Indian Penal Code, 1860 - Trial Court committed case filed under Section 376(2)(1) of Code to Fast Track Court - High Court dismissed petition for transferring case to Special Court under POSCO Act - Hence, present appeal by Appellant - Whether mentally retarded person who had crossed 18 years could be included under Section 2(d) of Act - Whether victim was entitled for compensation.

Facts:

An First Information Report (FIR) was lodged against Respondent alleging that he had committed rape on Appellant and on the basis of the FIR, investigation was carried on and eventually charge sheet was laid for the offence under Section 376(2)(1) of Code before the Magistrate, who, in turn, committed the case to the special Fast Track Court. A petition was filed before High Court praying that the matter should be transferred to the Special Court under the Protection of Children from Sexual Offences Act (POCSO) as the functional age of the Appellant was hardly around 6 to 8 years and there was necessity for trial to be conducted in a most congenial, friendly and comfortable atmosphere and the proceeding should be videographed. The matter was finally disposed of and transfer of the case to the Special Court established under the Act was not allowed. Hence, present appeal by Appellant.

Hon'ble Apex Court Held, while dismissing/ allowing the appeal:
Dipak Misra, J.:

i. The purpose of referring to the statement of objects and reasons and the preamble of the POCSO Act was to protect the children from the sexual assault, harassment and exploitation, and to secure the best interest of the child. The Act recognizes the necessity of the right to privacy and confidentiality of a child to be protected and respected by every person by all means and through all stages of a judicial process involving the child.

ii. When two constructions were reasonably possible, preference should go to one which helps to carry out the beneficent purpose of the Act; and that apart, the said interpretation should not unduly expand the scope of a provision. Thus, the Court had to be careful and cautious while adopting an alternative reasonable interpretation. The acceptability of the alternative reasonable construction should be within the permissible ambit of the Act.

iii. It is the foremost duty of the Court while construing a provision to ascertain the intention of the legislature, for it is an accepted principle that the legislature expresses itself with use of correct words and in the absence of any ambiguity or the resultant consequence does not lead to any absurdity, there is no room to look for any other aid in the name of creativity. There was no quarrel over the proposition that the method of purposive construction had been adopted keeping in view the text and the context of the legislation, the mischief it intends to obliterate and the fundamental intention of the legislature when it comes to social welfare legislations. While interpreting a social welfare one has to be guided by the 'colour', 'content' and the context of statutes. The Judge had to release himself from the chains of strict linguistic interpretation and pave the path that serves the soul of the legislative intention and in that event, he should become a real creative constructionist Judge.

iv. The Act deals with various facets that were likely to offend the physical identity and mental condition of a child. The legislature had dealt with sexual assault, sexual harassment and abuse with due regard to safeguard the interest and well being of the children at every stage of judicial proceeding in an extremely detailed manner. The procedure was child friendly and the atmosphere as commanded by the provisions of the Act had to be congenial. The protection of the dignity of the child is the spine of the legislation.

v. The mentally retarded person has a right to proper medical care and physical therapy and to such education, training, rehabilitation and guidance as will enable him to develop his ability and maximum potential. He has a right to economic security and to a decent standard of living. Whenever possible, the person should live with his own family or with foster parents and participate in different forms of community life. He has a right to a qualified guardian when this is required to protect his personal well-being and interests. He has a right to protection from exploitation, abuse and degrading treatment. For the above reasons, the only conclusion that could be arrived at was that definition in Section 2(d) defining the term "age" could not include mental age.

vi. The State/District Legal Services Authority has to conduct an inquiry and award the adequate compensation by completing the inquiry. Had the Accused been alive, the trial would have taken place in a Court of Session. As the Accused has died and the victim was certified to be a mentally disabled person under the Act, the State Legal Services Authority should award the compensation.

Rohinton Fali Nariman, J. - Concurring view:

i. A reading of the Act as a whole makes it clear that the intention of the legislator was to focus on children, as commonly understood i.e. persons who were physically under the age of 18 years. Does the Judge put himself in the place of the legislator and ask himself whether the legislator intended a certain result, or does he state that this must have been the intent of the legislator and infuse what he thinks should have been done had he been the legislator. It is at this point that the Judge crosses the Lakshman Rekha and becomes a legislator, stating what the law ought to be instead of what the law is.

ii. A reading of the Objects and Reasons of the Act together with the provisions contained therein would show that whatever was the physical age of the person affected, such person would be a person with disability who would be governed by the provisions of the said Act.

iii. Thus, it was clear that viewed with the lens of the legislator that it would be a violence both to the intent and the language of Parliament if one would read the word "mental" into Section 2(1)(d) of the Act. Given the fact that it was a beneficial/penal legislation, one could extend it only as far as Parliament intended and no further.

CHAPTER SIX

Jarnail Singh Vs. State of Haryana, 2013

Hon'ble Judges/Coram:

P. Sathasivam and J.S. Khehar, JJ.

Relevant Sections:

Section Section 374 of Criminal Procedure Code, 1973; Section 366, 376(g) and 120-B of Indian Penal Code, 1860

No. of pdf Pages of the Original Judgment: 10

Equivalent Citation:

2013VII AD (S.C.) 313, 2013(128)AIC148, AIR2013SC3467, 2013(4)AJR477, 2013 (83) ACC 136, 2013ALLMR(Cri)2946, 2013ALLMR(Cri)2946(SC), III(2013)CCR194(SC), 2013CriLJ3976, 2013(3)Crimes278(SC), JT2013(9)SC374, 2013(2)N.C.C.431, 2013(3)RCR(Criminal)644, 2013(7)SCALE764, (2013)7SCC263, 2013(2)UC1430, MANU/SC/0626/2013

Case Notes:

Indian Penal Code, 1860 - Section 366 and 376(g) and 120-B-- Criminal Procedure Code, 1973--Section 374--Rape--Conviction and sentence--Validity--Appreciation of evidence--Recovered from the possession of accused--No contradiction in statement--Statement fully supported by medical version--Consideration of--Held--Where the judgment is based on proper appreciation of evidence there requires no interference at this stage--Appeal dismissed.

Facts:

i. The factual position on which the prosecution version is founded, commences with the passing of information by Savitri Devi (the mother of the prosecutrix VW-PW6), to her husband Jagdish Chander-PW8, on 26.3.1993, at about 6 AM. She informed her husband, that the prosecutrix VW-PW6 was missing from their residence. In this behalf it would be pertinent to mention, that on 25.3.1993 at about 10 PM, Jagdish Chander went to sleep in the "baithak" (drawing room) of their residence. Savitri Devi, the mother of the prosecutrix VW-PW6, along with the prosecutrix VW-PW6, and the other children (comprising of three sons, the prosecutrix VW-PW6 and one other daughter), went to sleep in the other rooms of the house. Savitri Devi, told her husband, that she suspected the Accused-Appellant Jarnail Singh, may be responsible for having taken away their daughter.

ii. Jagdish Chander-PW8, commenced to search for his daughter. During the course of the aforesaid search, the Accused-Appellant Jarnail Singh, who had his residence in the neighbourhood (of Jagdish Chander-PW8), was also found missing from his residence. The search for the prosecutrix VW-PW6 by her father, proved futile. It is therefore, that Jagdish Chander-PW8, made a complaint Exhibit PO on 27.3.1993 to the Sub-Inspector Incharge, Police Post, Jathlana. In his complaint, he described VW-PW6, as the elder of his two daughters. He gave out her age as about 16 years. He also alleged, that his daughter VW-PW6 had gone missing from their residence in the night intervening 25th and 26th March, 1993. He also alleged, that an amount of Rs. 3,000/- was missing from his house, which he assumed may have been taken away by his daughter VW-PW6, while leaving the house. In the complaint Exhibit PO, the needle of suspicion was pointed at the Accused-Appellant Jarnail Singh.

Hon'ble Apex Court Held, while dismissing/ allowing the appeal:

i. We have given our thoughtful consideration to the above noted submission, advanced at the hands of the learned Counsel for the Appellant. We, however, find no merit therein. It is not as if the prosecution version is entirely based on the statement of the prosecutrix VW-PW6. It would be relevant to mention, that her recovery from the custody of the Accused-Appellant Jarnail Singh from the house of Shashi Bhan, at Raipur, is sought to be established from the statement of Moti Ram-PW3. There can therefore be no room for any doubt, that after she was found missing from her father's residence on 25.3.1993, and after her father Jagdish Chandra-PW8 had made a complaint to the police on 27.3.1993, she was recovered from the custody of the Accused-Appellant Jarnail Singh. Thereafter, the prosecutrix VW-PW6 was subjected to medico-legal examination by Dr. Kanta Dhankar-PW1 on 29.3.1993 itself at 3.00 p.m. Dr. Kanta Dhankar-PW1, in her independent testimony, affirmed that she had been subjected to sexual intercourse, inasmuch as her hymen was found ruptured. Even though the visual examination of the prosecutrix VW-PW6, during the course of her medico-legal examination did not reveal the presence of semen or blood, yet the report of the forensic science laboratory (Exhibit PL) and of the Serologist (Exhibit PL/1) clearly establish the presence of semen on her salwar, underwear and pubic hair. The serologist's report also disclose, medium and small blood stains on her "salwar". In her own deposition, she had mentioned that, when she was raped by the Accused-Appellant Jarnail Singh and his accomplices, bleeding had taken place and she had felt pain, and her clothes were stained with blood. Her deposition stands scientifically substantiated by Exhibits PL and PL/1. The suggestion put to the prosecutrix VW-PW6 at the behest of the Accused-Appellant Jarnail Singh, during the course of her cross-examination, that she had accompanied the Accused-Appellant Jarnail Singh, of her own free will and had had sexual intercourse with him consensually, leaves no room for any doubt, that she was in his company, and that, he had sexual intercourse with her. The assertion that the prosecutrix VW-PW6 had accompanied the Accused-Appellant Jarnail Singh, and had had sexual intercourse with him consensually is completely ruled out, because as per the substantiated prosecution version, the prosecutrix VW-PW6 was not taken away by the Accused-Appellant Jarnail Singh alone, but also, by his three accomplices. All the four of them had similarly violated her person. Additionally, in her statement under Section 164 of the Code of Criminal procedure, the prosecute VW-PW6 had asserted, that in the first instance, after having caught hold of her, the Accused had made her inhale something from a cloth which had made her unconscious. Thereafter, when the Accused-Appellant Jarnail Singh attempted to commit intercourse with her, she had slapped him. He had then put a cloth in her mouth, to stop her from raising an alarm. Thereafter, each one of the accomplices had committed forcible intercourse with her in turns. The factum of commission of forcible intercourse by the Accused-Appellant, as also, his accomplices was reiterated by her during her testimony before the Trial Court as PW6. Besides the aforesaid, there is a statement of her own father, Jagdish Chandra (PW8) who also in material particulars had corroborated the testimony of the prosecutrix VW-PW6. The prosecutrix VW-PW6, was not subjected to cross-examination on any of these issues. Nor was the prosecutrix confronted with either the statements made by her under Section 161 or Section 164 of the Code of Criminal Prosecution, so as to enable her to explain discrepancies, if any. Therefore, we find no merit at all, in the submission advanced by the learned Counsel. In the above view of the matter, we are satisfied that there was substantial material corroborating the statement of the prosecutrix VW-PW6, for an unequivocal determination of the guilt of the Accused-Appellant Jarnail Singh.

ii. No other submission besides those dealt with hereinabove, was advanced at the hands of the learned Counsel for the Appellant. For the reasons recorded above, we find no merit in the instant appeal and the same is accordingly dismissed.

CHAPTER SEVEN

NIPUN SAXENA AND ORS. VS. UNION OF INDIA (UOI) AND ORS., 2018

Honb'le Judges/Coram:

Madan B. Lokur and Deepak Gupta, JJ.

Relevant Sections:

Section 228A, Sections 376, 376A, 376AB, 376B, 376C, 376D, 376DA, 376DB or 376E of Indian Penal Code, 1860

No. of pdf Pages of the Original Judgments: 17

Equivalent Citation:

2019(1)ACR663, 2019(194)AIC36, 2019 (106) ACC 981, 2019(1)BLJ1, 2019(1)BomCR807, 2019(1)BomCR(Cri)910, 127(2019)CLT719, 2019(1)J.L.J.R.75, 2019(1)JLJ178, 2019 (1) KHC 199, 2019(1)PLJR129, 2019(1)RCR(Criminal)334, 2018(15)SCALE769, (2019)2SCC703, 2019 (1) SCJ 430, MANU/SC/1459/2018

Case Notes:

Criminal - Rape victims - Protection therof - Section 228A of Indian Penal Code, 1860 (IPC) - In present case, issue was regarding protection of rape victims and non-disclosure of name and identity of a victim falling within purview of POCSO - How and in what manner identity of adult victims of rape and children who were victims of sexual abuse should be protected.

Facts:

In present matter, question raised was how and in what manner identity of adult victims of rape and children who were victims of sexual abuse should be protected so that they were not subjected to unnecessary ridicule, social ostracisation and harassment, was one of issues which arises in these cases. Present judgment was divided into two parts. First part dealt with victims of offence of rape under Indian Penal Code, 1860 ('IPC') and second part dealt with victims who were subjected to offences under Protection of Children from Sexual Offences Act, 2012 ('POCSO').

Hon'ble Apex Court Held, while dismissing/ allowing the appeal:

i. Vide Amendment Act of 1983 cases of rape, gang rape etc. were excluded from category of cases to be tried in open Court. Later other similar offences were included vide Amendment Act of 2013.

ii. Sub-section (1) of Section 228A of IPC, provided that, any person who made known name and identity of a person who was an alleged victim of an offence falling under Sections 376, 376A, 376AB, 376B, 376C, 376D, 376DA, 376DB or 376E commited a criminal offence and shall be punishable for a term which may extend to two years.

iii. What was however, permitted under Sub-section (2) of Section 228A of IPC was making known identity of victim by printing or publication under certain circumstances described therein. Any person, who published any matter in relation to proceedings before a Court with respect to such an offence, without permission of Court, commited an offence. Explanation however provided that printing or publication of judgment of High Courts or Supreme Court will not amount to any offence within meaning of IPC.

iv. Neither Indian Penal Code nor Code of Criminal Procedure define phrase 'identity of any person'. Section 228A of IPC clearly prohibited printing or publishing "the name or any matter which might make known identity of person". It was obvious that not only publication of name of victim was prohibited but also disclosure of any other matter which may make known identity of such victim. Phrase "matter which might make known identity of person" did not solely mean that only name of victim should not be disclosed but it also means that identity of victim should not be discernible from any matter published in media.

v. A victim of rape would face hostile discrimination and social ostracisation in society. Such victim would find it difficult to get a job, would find it difficult to get married and would also find it difficult to get integrated in society like a normal human being. Our criminal jurisprudence did not provide for an adequate witness protection programme and, refore, need was much greater to protect victim and hide her identity. Supreme Court held that, no person could print or publish name of victim or disclose any facts which could lead to victim being identified and which should make her identity known to public at large.

vi. Sub-section (2) of Section 228A of IPC made an exception for police officials who might have to record true identity of victim in police station or in investigation file. In first information report ('FIR') name of victim would have to be disclosed. However, this should not be made public and especially not to media. Copy of an FIR relating to offence of rape against a women or offences against children falling within purview of POCSO shall not be put in public domain to prevent name and identity of victim from being disclosed. Sessions Judge/Magistrate/Special Court could for reasons to be recorded in writing and keeping in view interest of victim permit copy of FIR to be given to some person(s). Police officials should keep all documents in which name of victim was disclosed in a sealed cover and replace se documents by identical documents in which name of victim was removed in all records which may be scrutinised by a large number of people. Sealed cover could be filed in court along with report filed under Section 173 of Code of Criminal Procedure.

vii. As far as Clause (b) of Sub-section (2) of Section 228A of IPC was concerned, if an adult victim had no objection to her name being published or identity being disclosed, she could obviously authorize any person in writing to disclose her name. This had to be a voluntary and conscious act of victim. There were some victims who were strong enough and willing to face society even after ir names were disclosed. Some of them, in fact, help other victims of rape and they become a source of inspiration to other rape victims. Nobody could have any objection to victim disclosing her name as long as victim was a major.

viii. This Court, more than two decades back in Gurmit Singh's case raised a note of caution. It found that, sexual crimes against women were rising. This Court held that victims of sexual abuse or assault were treated without any sensitivity during course of investigation and trial. Court further held that trial of rape cases in camera should be Rule and open trial an exception.

ix. Section 228A of IPC imposed a clear cut bar on name or identity of victim being disclosed. What happened if Accused was acquitted and victim of offence wanted to file an appeal under Section 372 of Code of Criminal Procedure? was she bound to disclose her name in memo of appeal? Such a victim could move an application to Court praying that, she may be permitted to file a petition under a pseudonymous name e.g. 'X' or 'Y' or any other such coded identity that she may choose. However, she might not be permitted to give some other name which might indirectly harm another person. There might be certain documents in which her name will have to be disclosed; e.g., power of attorney and affidavit(s) which may had to be filed as per Rules of Court. Court should normally allow such applicant to file petition/ appeal in a pseudonymous name. Where a victim files an appeal we direct that such victim can file such an appeal by showing her name as 'X' or 'Y' along with an application for non-disclosure of name of victim. Any documents disclosing name and identity of victim should not be in public domain.

x. A minor who was subjected to sexual abuse needs to be protected even more than a major victim because a major victim being an adult may still be able to withstand social ostracization and mental harassment meted out by society, but a minor victim will find it difficult to do so. Most crimes against minor victims were not even reported as very often, perpetrator of crime was a member of family of victim or a close friend. Efforts were made to hush up crime. It was now recognised that, a child needs extra protection. India was a signatory to United Nations Convention on Rights of Child, 1989 and Parliament thought it fit to enact POCSO in year 2012, which specifically dealt with sexual offences against all children.

xi. Supreme Court issued directions that, No person could print or publish in print, electronic, social media, etc. name of victim or even in a remote manner disclose any facts which could lead to victim being identified and which should make her identity known to public at large. In cases where victim was dead or of unsound mind name of victim or her identity should not be disclosed even under authorization of next of kin, unless circumstances justifying disclosure of her identity exist, which shall be decided by competent authority, which at present was Sessions Judge. FIRs relating to offences Under Sections 376, 376A, 376AB, 376B, 376C, 376D, 376DA, 376DB or 376E of IPC and offences under POCSO shall not be put in public domain. In case a victim files an appeal under Section 372 Code of Criminal Procedure, it was not necessary for victim to disclose his/her identity and appeal shall be dealt with in manner laid down by law. Police officials should keep all documents in which name of victim was disclosed, as far as possible, in a sealed cover and replace se documents by identical documents in which name of victim was removed in all records which may be scrutinised in public domain. All authorities to which name of victim was disclosed by investigating agency or court were also duty bound to keep name and identity of victim secret and not disclose it in any manner except in report which should only be sent in a sealed cover to investigating agency or court. An application by next of kin to authorise disclosure of identity of a dead victim or of a victim of unsound mind Under Section 228A(2)(c) of Indian Penal Code should be made only to Sessions Judge concerned until Government acts under Section 228A(1)(c) and laid down a criteria as per our directions for identifying such social welfare institutions or organisations. In case of minor victims under POCSO, disclosure of ir identity can only be permitted by Special Court, if such disclosure was in interest of child. All States/Union Territories were requested to set up at least one 'one stop centre' in every district within one year.

A copy of this judgment be sent to Registrar General of all High Courts so that same can be placed before Chairpersons of Juvenile Justice Committee of all High Courts for issuance of appropriate orders and directions and also to ensure that sincere efforts were made to set up one stop centres in every district. Petitions disposed off.

CHAPTER EIGHT

Labhuji Amratji Thakor and Ors. Vs. The State of Gujarat and Ors., 2018

Hon'ble Judges/Coram:

A.K. Sikri, Ashok Bhushan and Ajay Rastogi, JJ.

Relevant Sections:

Sections 363 and 366 of Indian Penal Code (IPC); Sections 3 and 4 of Protection of Children from Sexual Offences Act, 2012; Section 319 of Code of Criminal Procedure, 1973

No. of pdf Pages of the Original Judgment: 05

Equivalent Citation:

2019(195)AIC99, AIR2019SC734, 2019 (2) ALD(Crl.) 13 (SC), 2019 (3) ALT (Crl.) 51 (A.P.), 2019(1)BLJ106, 2019(1)BomCR(Cri)448, 2018(4)Crimes369(SC), 2018GLH(3)690, (2019)2GLR1168, 2019(1)J.L.J.R.168, 2019(2)JCC1268, 2018(4)MLJ(Crl)739, 2018(3)N.C.C.752, 2018(II)OLR1061, 2019(1)PLJR222, 2019(1)RCR(Criminal)1, 2018(15)SCALE39, (2019)12SCC644, 2019 (3) SCJ 641, 2018(3)UC2156, MANU/SC/1302/2018

Case Note:

Criminal - Proceedings - Quashing of - Sections 363 and 366 of Indian Penal Code (IPC); Sections 3 and 4 of Protection of Children from Sexual Offences Act, 2012 ("POCSO ACT"); Section 319 of Code of Criminal Procedure, 1973 (CrPC) - Present appeal was filed by Appellants challenging judgment of High Court by which judgment Criminal Revision Application filed by complainant-Respondent No. 2 had been allowed by setting aside order of Additional District & Sessions Judge, who had rejected application filed by prosecution for proceeding against Appellants in Special POCSO Case - Whether High Court committed error in setting aside order of trial Court rejecting application under Section 319 of CrPC.

Facts:

In instant matter, complainant-Respondent No. 2 lodged a First Information Report under Sections 363 and 366 of IPC and under Sections 3 and 4 of POCSO ACT. An application under Section 319 of CrPC was filed by Additional Public Prosecutor, where it was stated that, in statement of victim, PW4, she had taken name of Labhuji, Shashikant and Jituji also, who had taken victim to Morbi in jeep. Prayer was made to proceed against Appellants also by initiating appropriate legal proceedings. Learned POCSO Judge after considering the submissions of parties rejected application. POCSO Judge also observed that, prima facie it appeared that with mala fide intention, names of Appellants had been disclosed. Complainant filed a Criminal Revision against order rejecting application, which had been allowed by High Court by impugned judgment. Aggrieved with said judgment, Appellants had come up in this appeal.

Hon'ble Apex Court Held, while dismissing/ allowing the appeal:

i. Section 319 of CrPC provided that where, in course of any inquiry into, or trial of, an offence, it appeared from evidence that, any person not being Accused had committed any offence for which such person could be tried together with Accused, Court might proceed against such person for offence which he appeared to have committed. Court, thus, during trial on basis of any evidence was fully empowered to proceed against any person, whose name was not even included in F.I.R. or Charge Sheet. Parameters of exercise of power under Section 319 of CrPC had been explained by present Court time and again.

ii. Constitution Bench in Hardeep Singh had held that, under Section 319 of CrPC, Court could proceed against any person, who was not an Accused in a case before it. Constitution Bench, however, has held that, person against whom Court decided to proceed, "had to be a person whose complicity might be indicated and connected with commission of offence"

iii. Constitution Bench had given a caution that, power under Section 319 of CrPC was a discretionary and extraordinary power, which should be exercised sparingly and only in those cases where circumstances of case so warrant. Crucial test, which had been laid down was "test that had to be applied was one which was more than prima facie case as exercised at time of framing of charge, but short of satisfaction to an extent that, evidence, if went unrebutted, would lead to conviction." Present was a case, where trial Court had rejected application filed by prosecution under Section 319 of CrPC. Further, in present case, complainant in F.I.R. had not taken the names of Appellants and after investigation in which statement of victim was also recorded, names of Appellants did not figure. After carrying investigation, tCharge Sheet was submitted in which Appellants names were also not mentioned as Accused.

iv. In present case, there were not even suggestion of any act done by Appellants amounting to an offence referred to in Sections 3 and 4 of POCSO Act. Thus, there was no occasion to proceed against the Appellants under POCSO Act.

v. High Court did not even record any satisfaction that, evidence on record as revealed by statement of victim and her mother even makes out a prima facie case of offence against Appellants. Mere fact that Court had power under Section 319 CrPC to proceed against any person who was not named in F.I.R. or in Charge Sheet did not mean that, whenever in a statement recorded before Court, name of any person was taken, Court had to mechanically issue process under Section 319 of CrPC. Regarding statement of victim, PW4, she had only stated that Natuji, Accused had come along with his three friends, i.e. Appellants and she was taken in jeep. She did not even alleged complicity of Appellants in the offence. Mere fact that jeep, in which she was taken to Modasa, Appellants were also present could not be treated to be any allegation of complicity of Appellants in offence.

High Court committed error in setting aside order of trial court rejecting application under Section 319 of CrPC. High Court had not given sufficient reasons for allowing application under Section 319 of CrPC filed by prosecution. Impugned judgment of High Court was unsustainable and was set aside. Appeal allowed.

CHAPTER NINE

Sachin Kumar Singhraha Vs. State of Madhya Pradesh, 2019

Hon'ble Judges/Coram:

N.V. Ramana, Mohan M. Shantanagoudar and Indira Banerjee, JJ.

Relevant Sections:

Sections 201(II), 302, 363 and 376(A) of Indian Penal Code, 1860

No. of pdf Pages of the Original Judgment: 07

Equivalent Citation:

2019(200)AIC64, AIR2019SC1416, 2019 (2) ALD(Crl.) 67 (SC), 2019 (108) ACC 1000, 2020 (2) ALT (Crl.) 54 (A.P.), 2019(2)BLJ462, 2019CriLJ2257, 2019(1)Crimes278(SC), 2019(2)JCC1375, 2020(1)JKJ324[SC], 2019(2)JLJ256, 2019(2)N.C.C.524, 2019(2)RCR(Criminal)351, 2019(5)SCALE39, (2019)8SCC371, 2019 (7) SCJ 202, MANU/SC/0352/2019

Case Note:

Criminal - Death sentence - Modification of - Sections 201(II),302,363 and 376(A) of Indian Penal Code, 1860 - First Additional Sessions Judge convicted Accused/Appellant for offences of murder, rape, etc punishable under Sections 363, 376(A), 302 and 201(II) of Code and Section 5(i)(m) read with Section 6 of Act, 2012 and sentenced him to death - Judgment of Trial Court was confirmed by High Court - Hence, present appeal - Whether impugned conviction and sentence of death warrant any interference.

Facts:

The First Additional Sessions Judge, convicted the Accused/Appellant for the offences of murder, rape, kidnapping, etc punishable under Sections 363, 376(A), 302 and 201(II) of the Indian Penal Code and Section 5(i)(m) read with Section 6 of the Protection of Children from Sexual Offences Act, 2012 and sentenced him to death. The judgment of the Trial Court was confirmed by the High Court, except in respect of the offence under Section 363 of Indian Penal Code which means the Accused was acquitted under Section 363 of Indian Penal Code by the High Court.

Ratio Decidendi:

The death sentence must be imposed only when life imprisonment appears to be an altogether inappropriate punishment, having regard to the relevant facts and circumstances of the crime.

Hon'ble Apex Court Held, while dismissing/ allowing the appeal:

i. The Trial Court as well as the High Court had rightly concluded that the prosecution has proved its case beyond reasonable doubt for the offence with which the Accused/Appellant was charged. All the circumstances relied upon by the prosecution are proved beyond reasonable doubt and consequently the chain of circumstances was so complete so as to not leave any doubt in the mind of the Court that it was the Accused and Accused alone who committed the offence in question. It was worth reiterating that though certain discrepancies in the evidence and procedural lapses had been brought on record, the same would not warrant giving the benefit of doubt to the Accused/Appellant. It must be remembered that justice could not be made sterile by exaggerated adherence to the Rule of proof, inasmuch as the benefit of doubt given to an Accused must always be reasonable, and not fanciful.

ii. Appellant had committed a heinous offence in a premeditated manner, as is indicated by the false pretext given to elder brother of victim's father to gain custody of the victim. He not only abused the faith reposed in him by the elder brother of victim's father, but also exploited the innocence and helplessness of a child as young as five years of age. This court was not convinced that the probability of reform of the Accused/ Appellant was low, in the absence of prior offending history and keeping in mind his overall conduct.

iii. Therefore, the crime in question may not fall under the category of cases where the death sentence was necessarily to be imposed. However, keeping in mind the aggravating circumstances of the crime, the sentence of life imprisonment simpliciter would be grossly inadequate in the instant case.

iv. Thus, we deem it proper to impose a sentence of life imprisonment with a minimum of 25 years' imprisonment (without remission). The imprisonment of about four years as already undergone by the Accused/Appellant shall be set off.

CHAPTER TEN

NAWABUDDIN VS. STATE OF UTTARAKHAND, 2022

Hon'ble Judges/Coram:

M.R. Shah and B.V. Nagarathna, JJ.

Relevant Sections:

Section 376(2) of Indian Penal Code, 1860; Sections 5 and 6 of the Protection of Children from Sexual Offences Act, 2012

No. of pdf Pages of the Original Judgment: 8

Equivalent Citation:

AIR2022SC910, 2022(1)Crimes 382(SC), 2022(1)RCR(Criminal)849, 2022(1)RLW630(SC), MANU/SC/0165/2022

Case Note:

Criminal - Conviction - Section 376(2) of the Indian Penal Code, 1860 (IPC) and Sections 5 and 6 of the Protection of Children from Sexual Offences Act, 2012 (POCSO Act) - Conviction directed by Trial Court upheld by High Court in appeal - Hence the present appeal - Whether the Accused/ Appellant was rightly convicted by the Courts vide judgments and orders impugned?

Facts:

The present appeal challenged the impugned judgment dismissing the appeal preferred by Accused-Appellant whereby confirming convictionof the Accused. By the detailed impugned judgment and order, the High Court has dismissed the said appeal and has confirmed the conviction of the Accused and the sentence of life imprisonment. Accused was aged approximately 65 years of age at the time of commission of offence. He was a neighbour of the victim girl who took advantage of the absence of her parents. He was found to have committed aggravated penetrative sexual assault on a girl child aged four years.Feeling aggrieved and dissatisfied with the impugned judgment of Trial Court and order passed by the High Court, the Accused preferred the present appeal.

Hon'ble Apex Court Held, while dismissing/ allowing the appeal:

The Accused-Appellant was the neighbour. The Accused instead of showing fatherly love, affection and protection to the child against the evils of the society, rather made her the victim of lust. It is a case where trust has been betrayed and social values are impaired. Therefore, the Accused as such does not deserve any sympathy and/or any leniency. However, the punishment provided for the offence under Section 6, as per the amended provision shall mean imprisonment for the remainder of natural life of that person, besides fine or with death. Accused is aged 70-75 years of age and it is also reported that he is suffering from Tuberculosis (TB). Therefore, considering such mitigating circumstances the life sentence is converted to fifteen years RI while fine imposed confirmed.

Impugned judgment and order passed by the High Court and the learned Special Court convicting the Accused upheld. The Accused is rightly held guilty for the aforesaid offences. Appeal partly allowed to the aforesaid extent only.

CHAPTER ELEVEN

Shatrughna Baban Meshram Vs. State of Maharashtra, 2020

Hon'ble Judges/Coram:
U.U. Lalit, Indu Malhotra and Krishna Murari, JJ.
Relevant Sections:
Sections 302, 376A and 376(1)(2)(f)(m) of Indian Penal Code, 1860 and Section 6 of Protection of Children from Sexual Offences Act, 2012
No. of pdf Pages of Original Petition: 65
Equivalent Citation:
2021ALLMR(Cri)715, 2021 (1) ALT (Crl.) 282 (A.P.), 2021(1)BomCR(Cri)1, 2021(1)J.L.J.R.414, 2020(6)JKJ190[SC], 2021(1)MLJ(Crl)38, 2021(1)N.C.C.437, 2021(1)PLJR434, (2021)1SCC596 MANU/SC/0822/2020
Case Note:
Criminal - Death sentence - Commutation of - Sections 302, 376A and 376(1)(2)(f)(m) of Indian Penal Code, 1860 and Section 6 of Protection of Children from Sexual Offences Act, 2012 - Appellant was tried by Trial Court for having committed offences punishable under Sections 376(1)(2)(f)(m), 376A, 302 of Code and under Section 6 of POCSO Act - Trial Court found that circumstances established guilt of Appellant and convicted Appellant - Trial Court, by its order passed on same day awarded Death Sentence to Appellant on two counts, i.e. under Section 302 of Code

and under Section 376-A of Code - High Court upheld conviction and sentence as recorded by Trial Court and confirmed Death Sentence - Hence, present appeal - Whether impugned death sentence awarded to Appellant warrant any interference.

Facts:

The Appellant was tried by the Trial Court in Special Case (POCSO Act) for having committed offences punishable under Sections 376(1)(2)(f)(m), 376A, 302 of Indian Penal Code and under Section 6 of the POCSO Act. The Trial Court found that the circumstances established the guilt of the Appellant. After declaring the Accused guilty for the offences punishable under Section 376(1)(2)(f)(i)(m) of Indian Penal Code, under Section 376-A of Indian Penal Code, under Section 302 of Indian Penal Code, and under Section 6 of Protection of Children from Sexual Offences Act, the Trial Court by its order passed on the same day awarded Death Sentence to the Appellant on two counts, i.e. under Section 302 of Indian Penal Code and under Section 376-A of Indian Penal Code; Rigorous Imprisonment for life under two counts, i.e. Section 376(1)(2)(f), (i) and (m) of Indian Penal Code and under Section 6 of POCSO Act. The Death Sentence was subject to confirmation by the High Court. The High Court upheld the conviction and sentence as recorded by the Trial Court and confirmed the Death Sentence.

Hon'ble Apex Court Held, while dismissing/ allowing the appeal:

(i)According to the prosecution, on the day in question when the victim was with her grandfather, on the pretext that the father of the victim had asked the Appellant to bring the victim, the Appellant, who was maternal uncle of the victim, took her away. This part of the evidence was conclusively established through the testimony of the grandfather. This version finds mention in the FIR which was recorded within few hours of the incident and in the statement of grandfather recorded under Section 164 of the Code. There was nothing on record to doubt the veracity of said version. It was true that some other witnesses were not examined by the prosecution but the strength of the testimony of grand father did not get diminished on any count nor can it be said that his testimony loses its weight because the witness was the grandfather of the victim. The version coming through this witness is cogent, consistent and also figured in prompt reporting of the FIR. Therefore, no hesitation in accepting that the first circumstance as noted by the Trial Court stands conclusively established.

(ii)As deposed by prosecution witnesses, the Appellant was found by the side of the victim at the spot. The victim was having various injuries whereafter she was taken for medical attention. Soon after the incident, the Appellant was also medically examined and Report showed injury on his body. Even if PW9 had turned hostile and some other witnesses were not examined, the fact that the victim was always in the custody of Appellant till she was found at the spot alongside the Appellant was quite clear. The proximity in terms of time and the promptitude in reporting were crucial factors and the evidence in that behalf was completely trustworthy. Thus, the second and third circumstances were also fully established.

(iii) Soon after his arrest, the Appellant was produced for medical examination before doctor, who found injury on private parts of the Appellant. The approximate time of said injury as given in the opinion was consistent with the case of prosecution. The submission however was that the Appellant was also examined by another medical professional and that report was not placed on record. The reference to the medical examination of the Appellant in terms of Section 53A of the Code was not to any other medical professional but to doctor. No explanation, not even a suggestion came from the Appellant how there could be an injury on his body as noticed in Report.

(iv) It must be stated that as per record, the chappals were not proved to be that of the Appellant and the pieces of flesh found at the spot of incident were also not proved to be that of a human being. However, the fact that the pant of the victim was found at the spot of incident is well established on record, and the circumstance must be taken to be proved only with respect to the recovery of the pant of the victim.

(v) There was nothing on record to show that the stains of semen found on clothing referred to in sixth circumstance, were medically proved to be that of, or could be associated with the Appellant. The sixth circumstance could not therefore be taken to be pointing against the Appellant.

(vi) It was true that the injuries on the lips of the victim showed that the margins were clean cut and given the nature of evidence in that behalf, it could not be said with certainty that those injuries could be taken to be the result of human bites. But the other injuries on the body of the victim were definitely by human bites and as such the absence of clarity with regard to the injuries on the lips did not render the case of the prosecution doubtful in any manner. Again, the absence of association of vaginal, cervical and anal swabs with the Appellant did not in any way diminish the strength of evidence against the Appellant.

(vii) The circumstances proved on record were not only conclusive in nature but completely support the case of the prosecution and were consistent with only one hypothesis and that was the guilt of the Appellant. They form a chain, so complete, consistent and clear, that no room for doubt or ground arises pointing towards innocence of the Appellant. It was, therefore, established beyond any shadow of doubt that the Appellant committed the acts of rape and sexual assault upon the victim and that injury was the cause of death of the victim.

(viii) The Appellant was thus guilty of having committed offences punishable under Clauses (f), (i) and (m) of Sub-section (2) of Section 376 of Indian Penal Code and also, under Clauses (j) and (m) of Section 5 read with Section 6 of the POCSO Act. Since according to medical opinion, the death was because of injury, the Appellant was also guilty of having committed offence punishable under Section 376A of Indian Penal Code.

(ix) Considering the age of the victim in the present case, the Accused must have known the consequence that his sexual assault on a child would cause death or such bodily injury as was likely to cause her death. The instant matter thus comes within the parameters of Clause fourthly to Section 300 Indian Penal Code and the question posed at the beginning of the discussion on this issue must be answered against the Appellant. The Appellant was therefore guilty of having committed the offence of culpable homicide amounting to murder.

(x) Though the Appellant was guilty of the offence punishable under Section 302 Indian Penal Code, since there was no requisite intent as would bring the case under any of the first three clauses of Section 300 Indian Penal Code, the offence in the present case did not deserve death penalty.

(xi) The offence was committed and just few days before such commission, Section 376A was inserted in Indian Penal Code by the Ordinance. The ex-post facto effect given to Section 376A inserted by the Amendment Act would not in any way be inconsistent with Sub-Article (1) of Article 20 of the Constitution. The Appellant is thus definitely guilty of the offence punishable under Section 376A Indian Penal Code. But the question remains whether punishment lesser than death sentence gets ruled out or not. As against Section 302 Indian Penal Code while dealing with cases under Section 376A Indian Penal Code, a wider spectrum is available for consideration by the Courts as to the punishment to be awarded. On the basis of the same aspects that weighed while considering the appropriate punishment for the offence under Section 302 Indian Penal Code, in view of the fact that Section 376A Indian Penal Code was brought on the statute book just few days before the commission of the offence, the Appellant did not deserve death penalty for said offence. At the same time, considering the nature and enormity of the offence, it must be observed that the appropriate punishment for the offence under Section 376A Indian Penal Code must be rigorous imprisonment for a term of twenty five years.

(xii) Consequently, while affirming the view taken by the Courts below in recording conviction of the Appellant for the offences punishable under Sections 302 Indian Penal Code and 376A Indian Penal Code, this court commute the sentence to life imprisonment for the offence punishable under Section 302 Indian Penal Code and to that of rigorous imprisonment for twenty five years for the offence punishable under Section 376A Indian Penal Code. The conviction and sentence recorded by the Courts below for the offences punishable under Section 376(1), (2)(f), (i) and (m) of Indian Penal Code, and under Section 6 of the POCSO Act were affirmed.

CHAPTER TWELVE

BARUN CHANDRA THAKUR VS. CENTRAL BUREAU OF INVESTIGATION AND ORS., 2017

Hon'ble Judges/ Coram:

R.K. Agrawal and Abhay Manohar Sapre, JJ.

Relevant Sections:

Sections 34 and 302 of Indian Penal Code, 1860 - Section 25 of Arms Act, 1959 - Section 75 of Juvenile Justice Act, 2000 - Section 12 of Protection of Children from Sexual Offences Act, 2012

No. of pdf Pages of the Original Judgment: 07

Equivalent Citation:

2018(182)AIC53, AIR2017SC5735, 2018 (1) ALD(Crl.) 23 (SC), 2018 (102) ACC 662, I(2018)CCR64(SC), 2018(1)Crimes51(SC), 2018(3)ECrN 844, 2018(1)JCC16, 2018(1)N.C.C.510, 2017(14)SCALE166, (2018)12SCC119, 2018 (1) SCJ 424 MANU/SC/1576/2017

Case Note:

Criminal - Grant of interim bail - Maintainability thereof - Sections 34 and 302 of Indian Penal Code, 1860 - Section 25 of Arms Act, 1959 - Section 75 of Juvenile Justice Act, 2000 - Section 12 of Protection of Children from Sexual Offences Act, 2012 - Petition was filed by Respondent for grant of interim bail - High Court granted interim bail for offences punishable under Sections of different Acts - Present appeal filed against order of High Court whereby High Court had granted interim bail to Respondents till presentation of challan subject to certain conditions - Whether order granting interim bail to Respondents was maintainable.

Facts:

Petition was filed by Respondent for grant of interim bail. High Court granted interim bail for the offences punishable under Sections 302 read with Section 34 of Code, Section 25 of Arms Act, Section 75 of the JJ Act and Section 12 of POCSO, Act, 2012 till next date on their furnishing bonds to the satisfaction of Investigation Agency. Appellants filed special leave petition to High Court which was disposed off making absolute the interim bail granted to Respondents till presentation of the challan subject to certain conditions. Hence, present appeal was filed by Appellants.

Hon'ble Apex Court Held, while dismissing/ allowing the appeal:

(i) Respondents could not be held guilty of any suppression, concealment or fraud for the simple reason that the petitions were prepared and accepted by the Registry of High Court. The fact relating to the withdrawal of the Resolution passed by the District Bar Associations could not be said to be in the knowledge of Respondents.

(ii) CBI was yet to examine and analyse the role of the Respondents and there was no evidence of their complicity in the crime and there was not even a pointer of involvement of Respondents in the alleged crime. Their involvement could no be established until and unless, there was some substantial evidence against them. High Court while granting interim bail to Respondents till the presentation of Challan had laid down conditions that Respondents should make themselves available for interrogation by the investigating agency as and when required and Respondents should not, directly or indirectly, make any inducement, threat or promise to any person acquainted with the facts of the accusation against them so as to dissuade him from disclosing such facts to the Court or to investigating agency. Respondents should not leave country without the prior permission of the Court.

(iii) Order passed by High Court granting interim bail to the answering Respondents till the presentation of Challan could not be faulted with.

45

CHAPTER THIRTEEN

KUMAR GHIMIREY VS. THE STATE OF SIKKIM, 2019

Hon'ble Judges/Coram:

Ashok Bhushan and K.M. Joseph, JJ.

Relevant Sections:

Sections 5(m),6,9 and 10 of Protection of Children from Sexual offences Act, 2012, Section 341 of Indian Penal Code, 1860 and Sections 386(b)(iii) and 401 of Criminal Procedure Code, 1973

No. of pdf Pages of the Original Judgment: 07

Equivalent Citation:

2019(199)AIC200, AIR2019SC2011, 2019 (2) ALD(Crl.) 818 (SC), 2019 (108) ACC 372, 2020 (3) ALT (Crl.) 72 (A.P.), 2019(3)BLJ185, 2020(4)BomCR(Cri)427, 2019CriLJ3141, (2019)4GLR2948, 2019(2)J.L.J.R.345, 2019(5)JKJ353[SC], 2019(2)KCCR1257, 2019(II)OLR528, 2019(2)PLJR358, 2019(2)RCR(Criminal)934, 2019(6)SCALE607, (2019)6SCC166, 2019 (6) SCJ 647 MANU/SC/0581/2019

Case Note:

Criminal - Alteration of sentence - Sections 5(m),6,9 and 10 of Protection of Children from Sexual offences Act, 2012, Section 341 of Indian Penal Code, 1860 and Sections 386(b)(iii) and 401 of Criminal Procedure Code, 1973 - Complaint was made to Police that Accused-Appellant, had attempted to sexually assault his seven year old daughter - FIR was registered and matter was taken up for investigation - Special Judge after considering entire evidence convicted Appellant under Section 9/10 of POCSO Act, 2012 as well as Section 341 of Code - On appeal before High Court, High Court dismissed appeal and altered conviction imposed under Section 9/10 of POCSO Act, 2012 to Section 5(m) read with Section 6 of Act and enhanced punishment to rigorous imprisonment of ten years - Hence, present appeal - Whether impugned judgment of conviction and sentence awarded to Appellant warrant any interference.

Facts:

A complaint was made to police that the Accused-Appellant, had attempted to sexually assault his seven year old daughter. The FIR was registered, matter up taken for investigation and chargesheet was submitted. Special Judge after considering the entire evidence convicted the Appellant under Section 9/10 of POCSO Act, 2012 as well as Section 341 of Indian Penal Code. The appeal was filed by the Appellant in the High Court which appeal though had been dismissed by the High Court but while dismissing the appeal the High Court altered the conviction imposed by the Special Judge under Section 9/10 of POCSO Act, 2012 to Section 5(m) read with Section 6 of Act and enhanced the punishment to rigorous imprisonment of ten years.

Hon'ble Apex Court Held, while dismissing/ allowing the appeal:

(i) The High Court can also exercise its power under Section 401 of Code of Criminal Procedure in an appropriate case. Section 401 of Code of Criminal Procedure provides for the power of revision to the High Court. The High Court could have very well exercised power under Section 401 of Code of Criminal Procedure read with Section 386(b) (iii)of Criminal Procedure Code, could have enhanced the sentence but the said course is permissible only after giving notice of enhancement.

(ii) The judgment of the High Court in so far as it enhanced the sentence from seven years to ten years was not in accordance with the procedure prescribed. The judgment of the High Court to the extent it had enhanced the sentence from seven years to ten years was set aside.

(iii) The victim herself appeared. She was thoroughly cross-examined by the Accused, the evidence of victim has proved, the charge levelled against the Accused which evidence was corroborated by evidence of prosecution witnesses who were also students studying in the same school and returning from the school at the time when victim was returning from the school. The medical evidence also fully corroborated the charge on the Appellant. The High Court had rightly affirmed the finding of the conviction of the Appellant. There was no ground to interfere with the finding of conviction and in fact the Appellant had not very seriously challenged the conviction of the Appellant. His submission was that he could have been awarded only sentence of five years under Section 10 of Act. The Special Judge after considering the factors imposed the sentence of seven years. The Special Judge had noted that the offence committed against the minor girl child could not be viewed lightly, fully endorse the view of the Special Judge and considering the serious nature of the offence the conviction of seven years rigorous imprisonment need no interference in this appeal. Thus, reject the submission of the Appellant that the sentence awarded ought to be reduced to five

CHAPTER FOURTEEN

Shamsher Singh Verma Vs.State of Haryana, 2015

Hon'ble Judges/Coram:

Dipak Misra and Prafulla C. Pant, JJ.

Relevant Sections:

Section 294 of Code of Criminal Procedure, 1973, Offence under Section 354 of Indian Penal Code - One relating to Protection of Children from Sexual Offences Act, 2015

No. of pdf Pages of the Original Judgment: 05

Equivalent Citation:

2015XII AD (S.C.) 594, 2016(158)AIC241, 2016 (1) ALD(Crl.) 275 (SC), 2016 (92) ACC 981, 2015ALLMR(Cri)4923, IV(2015)CCR303(SC), 2016(1)CLJ(SC)142, 2016CriLJ364, 2015(4)Crimes353(SC), 2015GLH(3)790, 2016(1)J.L.J.R.83, 2016(1)JCC42(SC), 2015(4)KLJ741, 2015(4)KLT1031(SC), 2016-2-LW(Crl)47, (2015) 4 MLJ(Crl) 618 (SC), 2016(1)N.C.C.53, 2016(I)OLR407, 2016(1)PLJR249, 2016(1)RCR(Criminal)167, 2015(12)SCALE597, (2016)15SCC485, 2015(3)UC2246, 2016(1)UC543 MANU/SC/1345/2015

Case Note:

Criminal - Application under Section 294 - Code of Criminal Procedure, 1973 - Report lodged against Appellant - Offence under Section 354 - Indian Penal Code - One relating to Protection of Children from Sexual Offences Act, 2015 - Charge sheet filed against Appellant - Statement of Accused recorded - Section 313 of Code of Criminal Procedure - Accused moved an application Under Section 294 - Code of Criminal Procedure - Rejected by Trial Court - Rejection affirmed by High Court - Present appeal - Whether the lower courts erred in not allowing the application of the Accused to get played the compact disc relating to alleged conversation between victim's father and son and wife of the Appellant regarding alleged property dispute - Whether the accused has been denied the right of defence

Facts:

A report was lodged against the Appellant (accused) at Police Station in respect of offence punishable under Section 354 of the Indian Penal Code, 1860 (Indian Penal Code) and one relating to Protection of Children from Sexual Offences Act, 2015 (POCSO) in which complainant alleged that his minor niece was molested by the Appellant. After investigation, a charge sheet was filed against the Appellant, on the basis of which Sessions Case was registered. Special Judge, after hearing the parties, framed charge in respect of offences punishable Under Sections 354A and 376 Indian Penal Code and also in respect of offence punishable Under Sections 4/12 of POCSO. Statement of the accused was recorded Under Section 313 of the Code of Criminal Procedure, 1973 (Code of Criminal Procedure).

In defence, the Accused moved an application Under Section 294 Code of Criminal Procedure before the trial court to play the compact disc relating to conversation between father of the victim and son and wife of the Appellant regarding alleged property dispute. The application was opposed by the prosecution. Consequently, the trial court rejected the same. The same was affirmed by High Court. The present appeal is against the said order of the High Court.

Hon'ble Apex Court Held, while dismissing/ allowing the appeal:

The object of Section 294 Code of Criminal Procedure is to accelerate pace of trial by avoiding the time being wasted by the parties in recording the unnecessary evidence. Where genuineness of any document is admitted, or its formal proof is dispensed with, the same may be read in evidence.

In view of the definition of 'document' in Evidence Act, and the law laid down by this Court, the Court held that the compact disc is also a document. It is not necessary for the court to obtain admission or denial on a document Under Sub-section (1) to Section 294 Code of Criminal Procedure personally from the accused or complainant or the witness. The endorsement of admission or denial made by the counsel for defence, on the document filed by the prosecution or on the application/report with which same is filed, is sufficient compliance of Section 294 Code of Criminal Procedure. Similarly on a document filed by the defence, endorsement of admission or denial by the public prosecutor is sufficient and defence will have to prove the document if not admitted by the prosecution. In case it is admitted, it need not be formally proved, and can be read in evidence. In a complaint case such an endorsement can be made by the counsel for the complainant in respect of document filed by the defence.

The Court is not inclined to go into the truthfulness of the conversation sought to be proved by the defence but, in the facts and circumstances of the case, as discussed above, the Court was of the view that the courts below have erred in law in not allowing the application of the defence to get played the compact disc relating to conversation between father of the victim and son and wife of the Appellant regarding alleged property dispute. In Court's opinion, the courts below have erred in law in rejecting the application to play the compact disc in question to enable the public prosecutor to admit or deny, and to get it sent to the Forensic Science Laboratory, by the defence. The Appellant is in jail and there appears to be no intention on his part to unnecessarily linger the trial, particularly when the prosecution witnesses have been examined.

Therefore, without expressing any opinion as to the final merits of the case, this appeal is allowed, and the orders passed by the courts below are set aside. The application dated 19.2.2015 shall stand allowed. However, in the facts and circumstances of the case, it is observed that the accused/ Appellant shall not be entitled to seek bail on the ground of delay of trial.

CHAPTER FIFTEEN

RAVI VS. THE STATE OF MAHARASHTRA, 2019

Hon'ble Judges/Coram:

Rohinton Fali Nariman, Surya Kant and R. Subhash Reddy, JJ.

Relevant Sections:

Sections 302,363,376 and 377 of Indian Penal Code, 1860 - High Court confirmed death reference in Sessions Case decided by Additional Sessions Judge, in which Appellant having been found guilty of committing offences of murder, rape, etc punishable under Sections 302, 363, 376 and 377 of Code, had been awarded sentence of death under Section 302 of Code.

No. of pdf Pages of the Original Judgment: 27

Equivalent Citation:

2020(207)AIC77, AIR2019SC5170, 2020 (2) ALD(Crl.) 218 (SC), 2020 (110) ACC 980, 2019ALLMR(Cri)4873, 2020 (1) ALT (Crl.) 123 (A.P.), 2020(2)BLJ394, 2019(4)Crimes39(SC), 2019(13)SCALE412, (2019)9SCC622 MANU/SC/1368/2019

Case Note:

Criminal - Death sentence - Rarest of rare - Sections 302,363,376 and 377 of Indian Penal Code, 1860 - High Court confirmed death reference in Sessions Case decided by Additional Sessions Judge, in which Appellant having been found guilty of committing offences of murder, rape, etc punishable under Sections 302, 363, 376 and 377 of Code, had been awarded sentence of death under Section 302 of Code - Trial Court as well as High Court had concurrently held that case falls within exceptional category of rarest of rare cases where all other alternative options but to award death sentence, were foreclosed - Hence, present appeal - Whether instant case satisfies test of rarest of rare cases and falls in such exceptional category where all other alternatives except death sentence, were foreclosed.

Facts:

The High Court confirmed the death reference in the Sessions Case decided by the Additional Sessions Judge, in which the Appellant having been found guilty of committing offences punishable Under Sections 302, 363, 376 and 377 of the Indian Penal Code had been awarded the sentence of death under Section 302 of Indian Penal Code along with the sentence of rigorous imprisonment(s) of different durations with fine for the rest of offences. The Trial Court as well as the High Court had concurrently held that the case falls within the exceptional category of rarest of the rare cases where all other alternative options but to award death sentence, were foreclosed.

Hon'ble Apex Court Held, while dismissing/ allowing the appeal:

Surya Kant, J.

(i) There was overwhelming eye-witness account, circumstantial evidence, medical evidence and DNA analysis on record which conclusively proves that it was the Appellant and he alone, who was guilty of committing the horrendous crime in this case. Therefore, upheld the conviction of the Appellant.

(ii) The victim was barely a two-year old baby whom the Appellant kidnapped and apparently kept on assaulting till she breathed her last. The Appellant who had no control over his carnal desires surpassed all natural, social and legal limits just to satiate his sexual hunger. He ruthlessly finished a life which was yet to bloom. The Appellant instead of showing fatherly love, affection and protection to the child against the evils of the society, rather made her the victim of lust. It's a case where trust had been betrayed and social values are impaired. The unnatural sex with a two-year old toddler exhibits a dirty and perverted mind, showcasing a horrifying tale of brutality. The Appellant meticulously executed his nefarious design by locking one door of his house from the outside and bolting the other one from the inside so as to deceive people into believing that nobody was inside. The Appellant was thus in his full senses while he indulged in this senseless act. Appellant had not shown any remorse or repentance for the gory crime, rather he opted to remain silent in his 313 Code of Criminal Procedure statement. His deliberate, well-designed silence with a standard defence of false accusation reveals his lack of kindness or compassion and leads to believe that he could never be reformed. That being so, this Court could not write of the capital punishment so long as it was inscribed in the statute book.

(iii) Therefore, affirm the death sentence.

R. Subhash Reddy, J.

(i) It was clear that in a case of conviction based on circumstantial evidence, ordinarily the extreme punishment of death penalty should not be imposed. In a given case, guilt of the Accused was proved beyond reasonable doubt, by establishing chain of circumstances, resulting in conviction, such cases, by considering balancing aspects of aggravating and mitigating circumstances, in appropriate cases, death penalty can be imposed. But, at the same time ordinarily, if no special reasons exist, in a case of conviction based on circumstantial evidence, death penalty should not be imposed. In this case on hand, the conviction of the Appellant was mainly based on circumstantial evidence. Thus, the death sentence, imposed on him, was to be modified.

(ii) In this case on hand, the mitigating circumstances of the Appellant, dominate over the aggravating circumstances, to modify the death sentence to that of life imprisonment. Even as per the case of prosecution, the Appellant was under influence of liquor at the time of committing the offence, and there was no evidence on record from the side of prosecution, to show that there was no possibility of reformation and rehabilitation of the Appellant. Further, age of the Appellant was twenty five years at the relevant time and conviction is solely based on circumstantial evidence. Taking all such aspects into consideration, the death penalty imposed on the Appellant was to be modified to that of life imprisonment, for the offence under Section 302 Indian Penal Code.

CHAPTER SIXTEEN

GANESAN VS. THE STATE, 2020

Hon'ble Judges/Coram:

Ashok Bhushan, R. Subhash Reddy and M.R. Shah, JJ.

Relevant Sections:

Section 7 read with Section 8 of the Protection of Children from Sexual Offences Act, 2012 (POCSO Act)

No. of pdf Pages of the Original Judgment: 08

Equivalent Citation:

2021(217)AIC265, AIR2020SC5019, 2021 (1) ALD(Crl.) 412 (SC), 2021 (114) ACC 638, 2021(1)CGLJ474, 131(2021)CLT1015, 2020(4)Crimes395(SC), 2020(4)J.L.J.R.383, 2020(5)JKJ227[SC], 2021(1)PLJR44, 2020(4)RLW3199(SC), (2020)10SCC573, 2020 (9-10) SCJ 456, 2020(3)UC1718 MANU/SC/0763/2020

Case Note:

Criminal - Conviction - Sustainability - Section 7 read with Section 8 of the Protection of Children from Sexual Offences Act, 2012 (POCSO Act) - Trial Court sentenced three years imprisonment and compensation to victim - High Court due to no representation by Appellant in appeal appointed legal aid counsel - During arguments leniency sought by laying emphasis only on compensation - High Court vide impugned judgment maintained the imprisonment term but modified compensation direction - State was directed to pay the compensation and to later recover from Appellant once he attains sound position - Hence, the present appeal - Whether the impugned judgment rightly dismissed appeal on the issue of imprisonment by denying opportunity of being heard to Appellant? - Appellant submitted that no sufficient opportunity was given to the

Accused before passing the impugned judgment and order - State on the other hand contended that mere disposal of appeal within four days from the date of providing legal assistance to Accused does not amount to denial of fair and sufficient opportunity.

Facts:

The Appellant/ Accused was tried and convicted for the offence punishable under Sections7 and 8 of the POCSO Act directing imprisonment and compensation of Rs.One lac to the victim. Vide impugned judgment, High Court partly allowed the appeal and modified the judgment passed by the trial Court with respect to compensation only and modified the order to the effect that compensation amount would be paid by the State to the victim girl and thereafter if the State finds that the Accused has got sufficient means, the same can be recovered from the Accused under the Revenue Recovery Act. Appeal so far related to conviction and imposition of sentence was dismissed. Hence, the present appeal by Accused.

Ratio Decidendi:

In a case involving sexual harassment etc. the statement of the prosecutrix, if found to be worthy of credence and reliable, requires no corroboration

Hon'ble Apex Court Held, while dismissing/ allowing the appeal:

In the present case, PW2-mother of the victim had turned hostile. However, PW3-victim fully supported the case of the prosecution. She narrated in detail how the incident had taken place. She has been thoroughly and fully cross-examined. There was no good reason to not to rely upon the deposition of PW3-victim. There can be a conviction based on the sole testimony of the victim, however, she must be found to be reliable and trustworthy.

On evaluating the deposition of PW3-victim, her sole testimony found to be absolutely trustworthy and unblemished and her evidence is of sterling quality. In the facts and circumstances of the case, the learned trial Court has not committed any error in convicting the Accused, relying upon the deposition of PW3-victim. The learned trial Court has imposed the minimum sentence provided Under Section 8 of the POCSO Act. Therefore, the learned trial Court has already shown the leniency. At this stage, it is required to be noted that allegations against the Accused which are proved from the deposition of PW3 are very serious, which cannot be permitted in the civilized society. Therefore, considering the object and purpose of POCSO Act and considering the evidence on record, the High Court has rightly convicted the Accused for the offence under Section 7 of the POCSO Act and has rightly sentenced the Accused to undergo three years R.I. which is the minimum sentence provided Under Section 8 of the POCSO Act.

So far as the amount of compensation awarded by the learned trial Court is concerned, the High Court has modified the same and has directed the State to pay the compensation to the victim and thereafter to recover the same from the Accused under the provisions of the land revenue, if it finds that the Accused has sufficient means. The aforesaid has been taken care by the High Court by modifying the judgment and order passed by the learned trial Court.

Appeal dismissed.

CHAPTER SEVENTEEN

RAVI ASHOK GHUMARE VS. STATE OF MAHARASHTRA, 2019

Hon'ble Judges/Coram:

R. Subhash Reddy and Surya Kant, JJ.

Relevant Sections:

Offence committed punishable under Sections 302, 363, 376 and 377 of the Indian Penal Code (IPC)

No. of pdf Pages of the Original Judgment: 27

Equivalent Citation:

2019(4)BomCR(Cri)574, 2020(1)JKJ231[SC], 2020(1)N.C.C.1 MANU/SC/1658/2019

Case Note:

Criminal - Death Reference - Offence committed punishable under Sections 302, 363, 376 and 377 of the Indian Penal Code (IPC) - Appellant was awarded the sentence of death - Trial Court as well as the High Court concurrently held that the instead case fall within the exceptional category of 'rarest of the rare' cases where all other alternative options but to award death sentence were foreclosed - Whether capital punishment was rightly sentenced by the trial Court and High Court?

Facts:

The informant (PW 9), a fruit-seller, while was in selling fruits, was informed by his wife that their daughter, who was 2 years old, was missing. He along with his relatives started looking for the child. During their search, the informant came to know that the Appellant was spotted drunk and was distributing chocolates to small children in the lane nearby. The informant went to the Appellant's house which was found locked. As the whereabouts of the missing child were still not known, the informant lodged a formal missing report to the police. The police reached Appellant's house which had two doors. One was found locked from outside while the other was locked from inside. Police broke open the door and entered the house along with the informant, his brother and a few other persons. They found the Appellant in the house; deceased-victim was lying under the bed in a naked and unconscious condition. Blood was oozing out from her private parts and had multiple injuries on her body. She was covered in a blanket and taken to the hospital where the doctor declared her brought dead. Inquest panchnama was prepared and the body was sent for post-mortem. A panel of doctors performed the post-mortem and found multiple injuries on the person of the victim. They opined that the death was caused due to throttling.

Hon'ble Apex Court Held, while dismissing/ allowing the appeal:

(i) There was overwhelming eye-witness account, circumstantial evidence, medical evidence and DNA analysis on record which conclusively proved that it was the Appellant and he alone, who was guilty of committing the horrendous crime. The conviction of Appellant was accordingly upheld.

(ii) Though the High Court had observed that 'satisfaction of lust' and 'removal of trace' was the Appellant's motive but motive is not an explicit requirement under the Indian Penal Code, though 'motive' may be helpful in proving the case of the prosecution in a case of circumstantial evidence. Lack of motive would not be fatal to the case of prosecution as sometimes human beings act irrationally and at the spur of the moment. The case in hand was not entirely based on circumstantial evidence as there were reliable eye-witness depositions who had seen the Appellant committing the crime, may be in part. Such an unshakable evidence with dense support of DNA test does not require the definite determination of the motive of the Appellant behind the gruesome crime.

(iii) The Sentencing Policy, therefore, needs to strike a balance between the two sides and count upon the twin test of (i) deterrent effect, or (ii) complete reformation for integration of the offender in civil society.

Where the Court is satisfied that there is no possibility of reforming the offender, the punishments before all things, must be befitting the nature of crime and deterrent with an explicit aim to make an example out of the evildoer and a warning to those who are still innocent. There is no gainsaying that the punishment is a reflection of societal morals. The subsistence of capital punishment proves that there are certain acts which the society so essentially abhors that they justify the taking of most crucial of the rights - the right to life.

(iv) The victim in the instant casewas barely a two-year old baby whom the Appellant kidnapped and apparently kept on assaulting over 4-5 hours till she breathed her last. The Appellant who had no control over his carnal desires surpassed all natural, social and legal limits just to satiate his sexual hunger. He ruthlessly finished a life which was yet to bloom. The Appellant instead of showing fatherly love, affection and protection to the child against the evils of the society, rather made her the victim of lust. It's a case where trust was betrayed and social values were impaired. The Appellant meticulously executed his nefarious design by locking one door of his house from the outside and bolting the other one from the inside so as to deceive people into believing that nobody was inside. The Appellant was thus in his full senses while he indulged in this senseless act. His deliberate, well-designed silence with a standard defence of 'false' accusation revealed his lack of kindness or compassion and leads to believe that he can never be reformed. Accordingly, capital punishment as imposed was confirmed.

R. Subhash Reddy, J. (Dissenting) (i) Views expressed to the extent of confirming the conviction recorded against the Appellant though was agreed, this was held as not a fit case where the Appellant could be awarded capital punishment and it required modification to that of the life imprisonment.

(ii) Further, the case on hand, rested solely on the circumstantial evidence. In a case of conviction based on circumstantial evidence, ordinarily the extreme punishment of death penalty should not be imposed. In a given case, guilt of the accused was proved beyond reasonable doubt, by establishing chain of circumstances, resulting in conviction, such cases, by considering balancing aspects of aggravating and mitigating, circumstances, in appropriate cases, death penalty can be imposed. But, at the same time ordinarily, if no special reasons exist, in a case of conviction based on circumstantial evidence, death penalty should not be imposed. In this case on hand, the conviction of the Appellant is mainly based on circumstantial evidence and hence death sentence should be modified.Appeal was allowed in part while upholding conviction and modifying sentence.

CHAPTER EIGHTEEN

SANGITABEN SHAILESHBHAI DATANTA VS. STATE OF GUJRAT, 2018

Hon'ble Judges/Coram:

N.V. Ramana and Mohan M. Shantanagoudar, JJ.

Relevant sections:

Sections 376(2)(f) and 376(2)(i) of Indian Penal Code, 1860; Sections 4, 5(c)(f)(m), 6, 8, 9(c)(f)(m),10, 23 and 33(7) of Protection of Children from Sexual Offences Act, 2012

No. of pdf Pages of the Original Judgment : 04

Equivalent Citation:

2019(1)J.L.J.R.16, 2018(4)KLT811, 2019(1)PLJR248, (2019)14SCC522 MANU/SC/1361/2018

Case Note:

Criminal - Bail - Validity of grant - Sections 376(2)(f) and 376(2)(i) of Indian Penal Code, 1860; Sections 4, 5(c)(f)(m), 6, 8, 9(c)(f)(m),10, 23 and 33(7) of Protection of Children from Sexual Offences Act, 2012 - FIR was lodged against Respondent No. 2 under Sections 376(2)(f) and 376(2)(i) of Code and Sections 4, 5(c)(f)(m), 6, 8, 9(c)(f)(m) and 10 of Act by Appellant - Respondent No. 2 was apprehended thereafter and Charge-Sheet was filed for offence mentioned in FIR - Respondent No. 2 approached High Court for bail and same was granted - Hence, present appeal - Whether High Court erred in granting bail to Respondent No.2.

Facts:

An FIR was lodged against Respondent No. 2 under Sections 376(2)(f) and 376(2)(i) of the Indian Penal Code and Sections 4, 5(c)(f)(m), 6, 8, 9(c)(f)(m) and 10 of the POCSO Act, by the Appellant, who was grandmother of the victim. Respondent No. 2 was apprehended thereafter and Charge-Sheet was filed for the offence mentioned in the FIR. Therein, Respondent No. 2 approached the High Court for bail and the same was granted.

Hon'ble Apex Court Held, while dismissing/ allowing the appeal:

(i) In the instant case, by ordering the scientific tests viz., lie detector, brain mapping and Narco-Analysis and venturing into the reports of the same with meticulous details, the High Court had converted the adjudication of a bail matter to that of a mini-trial indeed. This assumption of function of a trial court by the High Court was deprecated.

(ii) The concern of the legislature in protecting the identity of the victim was further evident from the provisions of POCSO Act. Section 33(7) of the same casts a duty on the Special Court to ensure that identity of the victim is not disclosed at any time during the course of investigation or trial. Further, Section 23 of POCSO Act provides restriction on any form of media to disclose the identity of the victim which tends to lower her reputation or infringes upon her privacy. No disclosure of any particulars is allowed which can eventually lead to disclosure of the identity of the victim.

(iii) Thus, taking note of the violation of settled principles of criminal law jurisprudence and statutory prescriptions vis-C -vis conversion of adjudication of bail application to a mini-trial and disclosure of identity of the victim by the High Court, this Court disapproves the manner in which the High Court had adjudicated the bail application and accordingly, quash the order passed by the High Court.

CHAPTER NINETEEN

ANOKHILAL VS. STATE OF MADHYA PRADESH, 2019

Hon'ble Judges/Coram:

U.U. Lalit, Indu Malhotra and Krishna Murari, JJ.

Relevant Section:

Sections 302,363,366,376(2)(f) and 377 of Indian Penal Code, 1860 and Sections 4,5 and 6 of Protection of Children from Sexual Offences Act, 2012

No. of pdf Pages of the Original Judgment: 20

Equivalent Citation:

2020(211)AIC90, AIR2020SC232, 2020 (1) ALT (Crl.) 101 (A.P.), 129(2020)CLT910, 2020(1)Crimes303(SC), ILR[2020]MP1011, ILR2020(1)Kerala1, 2020(1)J.L.J.R.245, 2020(4)JKJ368[SC], 2020(1)JLJ175, 2020 (1) KHC 79, 2020-2-LW(Crl)246, 2020(2)MLJ(Crl)389, 2020(1)N.C.C.654, 2020(1)PLJR289, 2020(1)RCR(Criminal)502 MANU/SC/1773/2019

Case Note:

Criminal - Death sentence - Expeditious disposal - Sections 302,363,366,376(2)(f) and 377 of Indian Penal Code, 1860 and Sections 4,5 and 6 of Protection of Children from Sexual Offences Act, 2012 - Charges were framed against Appellant for offences punishable under Sections 302, 363, 366, 376(2)(f) and 377 of Code and under Sections 4, 5 and 6 of Act - Accused had been convicted in charge of offence punishable under Section 363, 366, 376(2)(f), 377 and 302 of Code and Section 6 of Act and death sentence was awarded - Criminal Reference was registered in High Court for confirmation of death sentence - Appellant also preferred Criminal Appeal challenging his conviction and sentence - High Court affirmed view taken by Trial Court and upheld death sentence and other sentences imposed by Trial Court - Hence, present appeal - Whether there was any infraction or error on part of Trial Court in adopting approach in present matter and death sentence warrant any interference.

Facts:

The charges were framed against the Appellant for the offences punishable under Sections 302, 363, 366, 376(2)(f) and 377 Indian Penal Code and under Sections 4, 5 and 6 of Protection of Children from Sexual Offences Act, 2012. Accused had been convicted in charge of offence punishable under Section 363, 366, 376(2)(f), 377 and 302 Indian Penal Code and Section 6 of Protection of Children from Sexual Offences Act, 2012 and death sentence was awarded. Criminal Reference was accordingly registered in the High Court for confirmation of death sentence. The Appellant also preferred Criminal Appeal challenging his conviction and sentence. The High Court by its judgment and order presently under appeal, affirmed the view taken by the Trial Court and upheld the death sentence and other sentences imposed by the Trial Court.

Ratio Decidendi:

In the pursuit for expeditious disposal, the cause of justice must never be allowed to suffer or be sacrificed.

Hon'ble Apex Court Held, while dismissing/ allowing the appeal:

(i) The Amicus Curiae, was appointed and on the same date, the counsel was called upon to defend the Accused at the stage of framing of charges. One could say with certainty that the Amicus Curiae did not have sufficient time to go through even the basic documents, nor the advantage of any discussion or interaction with the Accused, and time to reflect over the matter. Thus, even before the Amicus Curiae could come to grips of the matter, the charges were framed. The concerned provisions viz. Sections 227 and 228 of the Code contemplate framing of charge upon consideration of the record of the case and the documents submitted therewith, and after hearing the submissions of the Accused and the prosecution in that behalf. If the hearing for the purposes of these provisions was to be meaningful, and not just a routine affair, the right under the said provisions stood denied to the Appellant.

(ii) The Trial Court on its own, ought to have adjourned the matter for some time so that the Amicus Curiae could have had the advantage of sufficient time to prepare the matter. The approach adopted by the Trial Court, in our view, may have expedited the conduct of trial, but did not further the cause of justice. Not only were the charges framed the same day as stated above, but the trial itself was concluded within a fortnight thereafter. In the process, the assistance that the Appellant was entitled to in the form of legal aid, could not be real and meaningful.

(iii) There were other issues which also arise in the matter namely that the examination of witnesses within seven days, the examination of the Accused under the provisions of the Section 313 of the Code even before the complete evidence was led by the prosecution, and not waiting for the FSL and DNA reports in the present case. DNA report definitely formed the foundation of discussion by the High Court. However, the record shows that the DNA report was received almost at the fag end of the matter, and after such receipt, though technically an opportunity was given to the Accused, the issue on the point was concluded the very same day. The concluding paragraphs of the judgment of the Trial Court show that the entire trial was completed in less than one month with the assistance of the prosecution as well as the defense, but, such expeditious disposal definitely left glaring gaps.

(iv) Therefore, set aside the judgments of conviction and orders of sentence passed by the Trial Court and the High Court against the Appellant and directing de novo consideration. It shall be open to the learned Counsel representing the Appellant in the Trial Court to make any submissions touching upon the issues whether the charges framed by the Trial Court are required to be amended or not, whether any of the prosecution witnesses need to be recalled for further cross-examination and whether any expert evidence was required to be led in response to the FSL report and DNA report. The matter shall, thereafter, be considered on the basis of available material on record in accordance with law.

Vijay Ranikwar Vs. State of Madhya Pradesh, 2019

Hon'ble Judges/Coram:

A.K. Sikri, S. Abdul Nazeer and M.R. Shah, JJ.

Relevant Sections:

Sections 201 and 376(2)(f) of Indian Penal Code, 1860 (Code) and Sections 5(i), 5(m),5(r) and Section 6 of Protection of Children from Sexual Offences Act, 2012 (POCSO Act)

No. of pdf Pages of the Original Judgment: 04

Equivalent Citation:

2019(201)AIC117, 2019(2)Crimes36(SC), 2020(1)JKJ286[SC], 2019(2)JLJ103, 2019(3)SCALE221, (2019)4SCC210, 2019 (7) SCJ 658 MANU/SC/0193/2019

Case Notes:

Criminal - Death sentence - Commutation of - Sections 201 and 376(2)(f) of Indian Penal Code, 1860 (Code) and Sections 5(i), 5(m),5(r) and Section 6 of Protection of Children from Sexual Offences Act, 2012 (POCSO Act) - Appellant was tried by Trial Court for offences punishable under Section 376(2)(f) and Section 201 of Code as well as Sections 5(i), 5(m) and 5(r) read with Section 6 of POCSO Act for having committed murder of minor girl after raping her - On considering incriminating material against Accused, Trial Court convicted Accused and sentenced Accused to death penalty - Having sentenced Accused with death penalty, Additional Sessions Judge made reference to High Court - Being aggrieved with conviction and sentence, Accused also preferred Criminal Appeal before High Court - High Court had decided reference against Accused and had also confirmed conviction and sentence of death penalty - Hence, present appeal - Whether death penalty imposed on Appellant warrant any interference.

Facts:

The Appellant/Original Accused was tried by the Trial Court for the offences punishable under Section 376(2)(f) and Section 201 of the Code as well as Sections 5(i), 5(m) and 5(r) read with Section 6 of the POCSO Act for having committed the murder of the minor girl after raping her. On considering the incriminating material against the Accused and on appreciation the evidences and having considered that the Accused was last seen together with the deceased and that the frock of the victim was found lying on the cot along with blood stains on bed mattress and bedsheet in the house of the Accused, which was not explained by the Accused, and also considering the medical evidence, the Trial Court convicted the Accused for the offences under Section 376(2)(f) and Section 201 of the Code as well as Sections 5(i), 5(m) and 5(r) read with Section 6 of the POCSO Act. The Trial Court sentenced the Accused to life imprisonment and other terms of the imprisonment with fine. All the sentences were directed to run concurrently. Additional Sessions Judge also sentenced the Accused to death penalty. Having sentenced the Accused with death penalty, the Additional Sessions Judge made the reference to the High Court. Being aggrieved with the conviction and the sentence, the Accused also preferred Criminal Appeal before the High Court. The High Court had decided the reference against the Accused and has also dismissed the criminal appeal preferred by the Accused, whereby, the High Court had confirmed the conviction and sentence imposed by the Trial Court.

Hon'ble Apex Court Held, while dismissing/ allowing the appeal:

(i) In the present case, prosecution had been successful in proving that the Accused was last seen together with the victim, that he gave one rupee coin to the victim, he told one of the witness who was with the victim to go away, thereafter the dead body of the victim was found near the house of the Accused and that the frock of the victim was lying on the cot and the bed mattress and bedsheet were blood stained and the same was matched with the blood group of the victim and that the Accused failed to explain the incriminating material/evidence found against him in the statement under Section 313 of Code of Criminal Procedure, 1973 the Trial Court had rightly convicted the Accused which had rightly been confirmed by the High Court. The Accused had failed to satisfy this Court how the findings recorded by the Trial Court, confirmed by the High Court, holding the Accused guilty for having committed the murder after raping a minor girl were perverse and/or contrary to the evidence on record. Therefore the judgment and order of the conviction passed by the Trial Court is confirmed.

(ii) So far as the request and the prayer made on behalf of the Accused to commute the death sentence to life imprisonment was concerned, the present case did not fall within the category of rarest of rare case warranting death penalty. This court had considered each of the circumstance and the crime as well as the facts leading to the commission of the crime by the Accused. Though, this court acknowledges the gravity of the offence, this court was unable to satisfy itself that this case would fall in the category of rarest of rare case warranting the death sentence. The offence committed, undoubtedly, could be said to be brutal, but did not warrant death sentence. It was required to be noted that the Accused was not a previous convict or a professional killer. At the time of commission of offence, he was nineteen years of age. His jail conduct also reported to be good. Considering the said mitigating circumstances and considering the decisions of this Court, it would be in the interest of justice to commute the death sentence to life imprisonment.

CHAPTER TWENTY-ONE

VIRAN GYANLAL RAJPUT VS. THE STATE OF MAHARASHTRA, 2018

Hon'ble Judges/Coram:
N.V. Ramana, Mohan M. Shantanagoudar and Hemant Gupta, JJ.
Relevant Sections:
Sections 302 and 201 of Indian Penal Code, 1860 (IPC); Sections 10 and 4 of Protection of Children from Sexual Offences Act, 2012 (POCSO Act)
No. of pdf Pages of the Original Judgment: 08
Equivalent Citation:
2019(198)AIC207, 2019ALLMR(Cri)784, 2019(1)BLJ189, 2019(1)BomCR(Cri)495, 2018(4)Crimes474(SC), 2019(1)N.C.C.111, 2019(1)RCR(Criminal)328, 2018(15)SCALE610, (2019)2SCC311, 2019 (3) SCJ 342, 2019 (1) WLN 124 (SC) MANU/SC/1420/2018
Case Notes:
Criminal - Death sentence - Sections 302 and 201 of Indian Penal Code, 1860 (IPC); Sections 10 and 4 of Protection of Children from Sexual Offences Act, 2012 ("POCSO Act") - Instant appeals had been filed against final common judgment of High Court whereby learned High Court confirmed death sentence awarded to Appellant herein - Whether death sentence awarded to Appellant was liable to be set aside.
Facts:

Case for prosecution in brief was that, when victim did not return home from school at usual time in evening, a search was undertaken. Next day, some of her belongings were found in jungle area adjoining village. A complaint (Exh. 14) regarding missing of girl was lodged. First information pertaining to offence of murder was given to police. Trial Court as well as High Court found following incriminating circumstances against Appellant, namely, deceased was last seen with him while she was walking home from school; Appellant was seen running alone towards Toranpada later in evening; recovery of dead body and incriminating articles (importantly, clothes of victim) at instance of Appellant; mud stains on pants of Appellant which matched with mud seized from spot of recovery of victim's body; failure of Appellant to explain injuries found on him; medical evidence showing that, victim had been forcibly raped and killed; motive to gratify lust, and to kill victim and hide her body to suppress evidence of his crime; and failure of Appellant to offer a plausible explanation for incriminating circumstances against him. Sessions Court had convicted Appellant for offences punishable under Sections 302 and 201 of IPC, and under Sections 10 and 4 of POCSO Act for kidnapping, rape and murder of a 13-year-old girl, and causing disappearance of evidence.

Ratio Decidendi:

Death penalty was to be imposed only when alternative of life imprisonment was totally inadequate.

Hon'ble Apex Court Held, while dismissing/ allowing the appeal:

1. Trial Court and High Court were correct in relying upon testimony of PWs 4 and 5, which was natural and reliable. Minor discrepancies in recorded timings and sequence of events pertaining to recovery of body, and articles including victim's schoolbag, as evident through First Information Statement (Exh. 63), testimony of I.O., PW14, and spot panchanama (Ex. 23), were not fatal to prosecution version and may be explained due to all events happening in quick succession, viz. apprehending of Appellant, recovery of dead body, lodging of FIR pertaining to murder and preparation of spot panchanama. Moreover, argument that recovery of dead body at instance of Appellant was highly suspicious could not be sustained, since it was clear from testimony of witnesses that body was recovered from a spot which could only have been within knowledge of person who hid body to begin with. This was also fortified by lack of any explanation by Appellant regarding recovery of body

and circumstance of victim being last seen around him. Medical evidence also clearly established occurrence of rape. Additionally, there were several scratch marks all over her body. As regards murder of victim, evidence of PW13 indicated that, she was killed by strangulation by red odhani which was found tied tightly around victim's neck when her body was recovered. Motive for crime, i.e. lust, was also apparent, which was an important consideration in cases based on circumstantial evidence, as pointed out by High Court.

2. Thus, each link in chain of circumstantial evidence had been adequately established by prosecution, and conviction of Appellant was affirmed.

3. Life imprisonment was Rule and death penalty was exception, and death penalty was to be imposed only when alternative of life imprisonment was totally inadequate, and therefore unquestionably foreclosed, i.e. if it was only inevitable conclusion, as per well-settled legal proposition first enunciated in Bachan Singh v. State of Punjab. While determining sentence, it was equally important for Court to consider aggravating circumstances of crime and mitigating circumstances of criminal. Moreover, since decision in Machhi Singh v. State of Punjab, a balancing approach of such aggravating and mitigating circumstances had been adopted, to see if crime was among rarest of rare cases. Though, crime committed was of an abominable nature, it could not be said to be of such a brutal, depraved, heinous or diabolical nature so as to fall into category of rarest of rare cases and invite punishment with death. Prosecution did not establish that, Appellant was beyond reform, especially given his young age. A sentence of life imprisonment simpliciter would not be proportionate to gravity of offence committed, and would not meet need to respond to crimes against women and children in most stringent manner possible. Possibility of reform of Accused was not completely precluded. In such a situation, it was deemed fit to restrict right of Appellant to claim remission in his sentence of life imprisonment for a period of 20 years.

4. Thus, Criminal Appeals were disposed of by commuting sentence of death awarded to Appellant to life imprisonment, out of which Appellant shall mandatorily serve out a minimum of 20 years without claiming remission.

Adv. Jayprakash Somani's Videos On Law

Adv. Jayprakash Somani's Videos on Law on Youtube- 'jaysomani64' channel.

1) SLP in Supreme Court / Special Leave Petitions in the Supreme Court of India

2) Transfer of Civil & Criminal Cases by the Supreme Court of India / Transfer of Matrimonial Cases

3) Appellate Jurisdiction of the Supreme Court of India

4) Jurisdictions of the Supreme Court of India

5) Public Interest Litigation in the Supreme Court of India / PIL in Supreme Court

6) Article 32 Writ Petitions in the Supreme Court of India

7) Bail Matters Top 10 Supreme Court Cases

8) FIR Quashing in High Court & Supreme Court

9) Bail & Anticipatory Bail Matters in Supreme Court

10) Insolvency & Bankruptcy Matters in the Supreme Court

11) Insolvency & Bankruptcy Code 2016 Part 1

12) Insolvency & Bankruptcy Code 2016 Part 2

13) Insolvency & Bankruptcy Code 2016 Part 3

14) Corporate Liquidation Process

15) Supreme Court Rules & Procedures Webinar of 2.5 hour on Zoom

16) RDDBFI Act, 1993 (Introduction)

17) The Indian Contact Act 1872

18) Negotiable Instruments Act (Introduction)

19) How to avoid matrimonial disputes& some more videos

20) SEBI Matters in the Supreme Court

21) Matrimonial Matters: Supreme Court's 20 Case Laws

22) Consumer Matters Supreme Court's 20 Case Laws

23) Service Matters Supreme Court's 20 Case Laws

24) How to Search Lawyer for Your Matter

25) Property Matters Supreme Court's 20 Case Laws

26) Bail Matters: Supreme Court's 20 Case Laws

27) Supreme Court / High Court Vacation Benches

28) 69000 Teacher's Recruitment Matters of UP Government in the Supreme Court

29) Contempt of Court Matters in the Supreme Court

30) Advocate Act's Matters in the Supreme Court

31) Business Law Matters in the Supreme Court

32) Banking Matters in the Supreme Court

33) Labour Law Matters in the Supreme Court

34) Arbitration Matters in the Supreme Court

35) Careers in Law -Zoom Webinar by Adv. Jayprakash Somani

36) Civil Matters in the Supreme Court

37) Consumer Protection Act | Consumer Matters in the Supreme Court

38) Corporate Matters in the Supreme Court

39) Criminal Matters in the Supreme Court

40) Role of Respondent in the Supreme Court of India

41) Motor Vehicle Accident Matters in Supreme Court with case laws

42) Article 131 Original Suits in Supreme Court

43) PIL in Supreme Court/ Public Interest Litigations in the Supreme Court of India'

44) CAB Citizenship Amendment Bill is not Unconstitutional

45) Supreme Court of India Cases & Process – Marathi

46) Legal Services Export / Export of Legal Services

47) Transfer of Matrimonial Cases by the Supreme Court of India

48) Public Interest Litigation PIL

49) The Specific Relief Act (Introduction)

50) Corporate Insolvency Resolution Process CIRP

51) ABMM's Career 5 - Careers in Law

52) Transfer of cases by Supreme Court

53) Writ Petitions in High Court & Supreme Court of India

54) Supreme Court Jurisdictions - Appeals, SLP, Writ Petitions, Transfer, Original, Review, Curative

55) LEGAL INDIA TV Show: Cases Handled in Supreme Court

56) Corporate Liquidation Process

57) Legal Services Export / Export of Legal Services

58) Corporate Laws

59) Election Matters- Supreme Court's 20 Case Laws

60) Companies Act, 2013

62) Competition Act, 2002

63) Banking Matters - Supreme Court's 20 Case Laws

64) Election Matters in the Supreme Court

65) Armed Forces Tribunal Matters in the Supreme Court

66) Compassionate Appointment Service matter

67) Foreign Exchange Management Act FEMA

68) Foreign Trade Policy 2021-26 Proposed

69) Customs Act 1962

70) Narcotic Drugs and Psychotropic Substances Act, 1985 NDPS Act

71) Foreign Trade Development & Regulation Act, 1992

72) How to Search Good Advocate in the Supreme Court of India

73) Sr. Adv Vikas Singh's Interview in Nani Palkhivala Wednesday Law Club

74) Indian Penal Code (I. P. C.)

75) Criminal Procedure Code (Cr. P. C.)

76) Commercial Courts & International Arbitration - by Mr. Jaideep Gupta, Senior Advocate in Nani Palkhivala Wednesday Law Club

77) Sr. Adv Ranji Thomos in Nani Palkhivala Wednesday Law Club

78) Urgent Matters in Supreme Court during vacations

79) 498A Bail Matters in Supreme Court

81) 376 Bail Matters in Supreme Court

82) 302, 304, 307, 308 Bail Matters in Supreme Court

83) 138, 420 Bail Matters in Supreme Court

84) POCSO Act Bail Matters in Supreme Court

85) NDPS Act Bail Matters in Supreme Court

86) What is ED (Enforcement Directorate)?

87) Prevention of Money Laundering Act, 2002 (PMLA Act)

88) Insolvency & Bankruptcy Code- Supreme Court Case Laws. Webinar in Nani Palkhivala Wednesday Law Club

89) What is NCLT & NCLAT?

90) Acquittal from 376- Supreme Court's some case laws in Nani Palkhivala Wednesday Law Club dt 28.7.22

91) Insolvency & Bankruptcy in India

92) Can we file case directly in the Supreme Court?

93) Adv. Anuja Pethia has cleared AOR Exam 2021 with 77% marks - Her interview in Nani Palkhivala Wednesday Law Club

94) Customs Act - Supreme Court Case Laws & Interview of AOR Adv. Anuja Pethia in Nani Palkhivala Law Club.

95) The Uttar Pradesh Public Service Tribunals Act, 1976

96) POCSO Act - Supreme Court Case Laws & Interview of AOR Adv. Shoumendu Mukharji & Adv. Nishant Verma in Nani Palkhivala Law Club.

97) Who Can Trigger CIRP Process Under Insolvency Law of India

98) The Uttar Pradesh Government Servant Discipline and Appeal Rules, 1999

99) CIRP Application Under Sec 7 by FC

100) Information Technology Act 2000

101) Uttar Pradesh Recruitment of Dependants of Government Servants Dying in Harness Rules, 1974

102) Foreign Exchange Management Act 1999 & Supreme Court's Case Laws on FEMA & Leading Case of AOR Exam in Nani Palkhivala Law Club.

103) Arbitration and Conciliation Act 1996 & It's Supreme Court Case Laws in Nani Palkhivala Wednesday Law Club.

104) Narcotic Drugs & Psychotropic Substances Act 1985 (NDPS Act) & It's Supreme Court Case Laws in Nani Palkhivala Wednesday Law Club.

105) Recovery of Debts and Bankruptcy Act 1993

106) Uttar Pradesh Land Revenue Code 2006

107) CIRP Application Under Sec 9 by OC

108) CIRP Application Under Sec 10 by CD

109) Hindu Succession Act, 1956

110) Maharashtra Civil Services Rules, 1981

111) Indian Contract Act, 1872 & Supreme Court's Case Laws" in Nani Palkhiwala Wednesday Law Club

112) Securities and Exchange Board of India Act, 1992 i. e. SEBI Act 1992 & Case Laws on Insiders Trading" in Nani Palkhiwala Wednesday Law Club

113) Moratorium Under Section 14 of IBC, 2016

114) Hindu Marriage Act, 1955

115) Maharashtra Land Revenue Code, 1966

116) 64 Leading Cases of AOR Exam Session 1 :- Cases 1 to16 in Nani Palkhiwala Wednesday Law Club

117) 64 Leading Cases of AOR Exam Session 2: Cases 17 to 32 in Nani Palkhivala Wednesday Law Club

118) 64 Leading Cases of AOR Examination Session 3: Cases 33 to 48 in Nani Palkhivala Wednesday Law Club

119) 64 Leading Cases of AOR Exam Session 4: Cases 49 to 64 in Nani Palkhiwala Wednesday Law Club

120) Labour Laws of India: Part 1 - 4 New Labour Law Codes of India

121) New Labour Laws Part 2 The Code on Wages, 2019

122) New Labour Laws Part 3:- The Code on Social Security, 2020

123) Argue in English Fluently & Confidently - Two months online course.

124) SLP Admission in the Supreme Court. 2023 (Hindi)

125) Transfer of Petitions from the Supreme Court (Hindi)

126) Review Petition in the Supreme Court.(Hindi)

127) Recovery of debts from the Company (Hindi)

128) How to search 'Good Insolvency & Bankruptcy Consultant?' (HINDI)

129) Curative Petition in the Supreme Court

130) AFT Appeals in the Supreme Court (HINDI)

131) NCLAT's Appeals in the Supreme Court.

132) Transfer Petition: Which matters can we transfer?

133) SLP Types of SLP in the Supreme court of India (English).

134) Argue in English Fluently and Confidently in the High Court & Supreme Court'.

List Of Adv. Jayprakash Somani's Published Books

1. Supreme Court of India's Leading Case Laws on 'Insolvency & Bankruptcy Code 2016'

2. Bail Matters – Supreme Court's Latest Leading Case Laws

3. Arbitration Matters- Supreme Court's Latest Leading Case Laws

4. Property Matters - Supreme Court's Latest Leading Case Laws

5. Matrimonial Matters- Supreme Court's Latest Leading Case Laws

6. Election Matters- Supreme Court's Latest Leading Case Laws

7. SEBI Matters- Supreme Court's Latest Leading Case Laws

8. Banking Matters- Supreme Court's Latest Leading Case Laws

9. Service Matters- Supreme Court's Latest Leading Case Laws

10. Contempt of Court Matters- Supreme Court's Latest Leading Case Laws

11. Consumer Protection Matters- Supreme Court's Latest Leading Case Laws

12. Corporate Law- Supreme Court's Latest Leading Case Laws

13. Supreme Court's AOR Exam- Leading Cases

14. Armed Force Tribunal - Supreme Court's Latest Leading Case Laws

15. Acquittal From 376 - Supreme Court's Latest Leading Case Laws

16. Negotiable instrument – Supreme Court's Latest Leading Case Laws

17. Contract Act- Supreme Court's Latest Leading Case Laws

18. Insider trading- Supreme Court's Latest Leading Case Laws

19. Foreign Exchange and Management Act- Supreme Court's Latest Leading Case Laws

20. Income Tax Act- Supreme Court's Latest Leading Case Laws

21. Company Law- Supreme Court's Latest Leading Case Laws

22. Competition & Monopoly Matters- Supreme Court's Latest Leading Case Laws

23. Compassionate Appointment- Service Matters- Supreme Court's Latest Leading Case Laws

24. Compulsory Retirement- Service Matters- Supreme Court's Latest Leading Case Laws

25. Voluntary Retirement- Service Matters- Supreme Court's Latest Leading Case Laws

26. Removal/Dismissal/Termination from Service- Supreme Court's Latest Leading Case Laws

27. Seniority- Service Matter- Supreme Court's Latest Leading Case Laws

28. Promotion- Service Matter- Supreme Court's Latest Leading Case Laws

29. Equal Pay for Equal Work- Service Matter- Supreme Court's Latest Leading Case Laws

30. Condition of Service- Service Matter- Supreme Court's Latest Leading Case Laws

31. Customs Act- Supreme Court's Leading Case Laws

32. Information Technology Act- Supreme Court's Leading Case Laws

33. SEC. 125 CR. P. C.- Supreme Court's Leading Case Laws

34. SEC. 498A OF I. P. C.- Supreme Court's Leading Case Laws

35. MOTOR VEHICLE ACT- Supreme Court's Leading Case Laws

36. CONDITION OF SERVICE- SERVICE MATTER- Supreme Court's Leading Case Laws

37. SUSPENSION- SERVICE MATTER- Supreme Court's Leading Case Laws

38. Reservation in SC, ST, OBC- Service Matter- Supreme Court's Leading Case Laws

39. NARCOTIC DRUGS AND PSYCHOTROPIC SUBSTANCES (NDPS) ACT - Supreme Court of India's Latest Leading Case Laws

40. SEC 302 IPC - Supreme Court of India's Latest Leading Case Laws

41. PROTECTION OF CHILDREN FROM SEXUAL OFFENCES ACT (POCSO) - Supreme Court of India's Latest Leading Case Laws

42. PMLA ACT BAIL MATTERS - Supreme Court of India's Leading Case Laws

43. SEC 376 BAIL MATTERS - Supreme Court of India's Leading Case Laws

44. SEC 302 BAIL MATTERS - Supreme Court of India's Leading Case Laws

45. POCSO ACT BAIL MATTERS - Supreme Court of India's Leading Case Laws

46. JUVENILE JUSTICE ACT- Supreme Court of India's Leading Case Laws

47. TRANSFER OF PROPERTY ACT- Supreme Court of India's Leading Case Laws

48. PROFESSIONAL ETHICS OF ADVOCATES- AOR EXAM- SUPREME COURT'S LEADING CASE LAWS

49. WHITE COLLAR CRIME- SUPREME COURT'S LEADING CASE LAWS

50. SEC 302 BAIL MATTERS- SUPREME COURT'S LEADING CASE LAWS

51. SEC 7 IBC 2016 - SUPREME COURT'S LATEST LEADING CASE LAW

52. ADVERSE POSSESSION IN PROPERTY MATTER - SUPREME COURT'S LATEST LEADING CASE LAWS

53. FOOD SAFETY AND STANDARD ACT 2006' - SUPREME COURT AND HIGH COURT's LEADING CASE LAWS

54. ARMED FORCE TRIBUNAL ACT- SUPREME COURT'S LATEST LEADING CASE LAWs

55. ESSENTIAL COMMODITIES ACT 1955- SUPREME COURT'S LATEST LEADING CASE LAWS

56. 'FOREIGN TRADE DEVELOPMENT AND REGULATION ACT'- SUPREME COURT AND HIGH COURT'S LEADING CASE LAWS

57. 'PARTNERSHIP ACT 1932'- SUPREME COURT'S LEADING CASE LAWS

58. 'COTPA ACT 2003' - SUPREME COURT AND HIGH COURT'S LEADING CASE LAWS

59. DOMESTIC VIOLENCE ACT 2005' - SUPREME COURT'S LEADING CASE LAWS

60. 'DOWRY PROHIBITION ACT 1961' - SUPREME COURT'S LATEST CASE LAWS

61.SUPREME COURT'S AOR EXAM- DRAFTING Formates of more than 25 Drafts for AOR Exam Paper 2 - Drafting

Books are available online in India

1. Notion Press: https://notionpress.com/author/jayprakash_somani

2. Amazon: https://www.amazon.in/s?k=jayprakash+somani

3. Flipkart: https://www.flipkart.com/search?q=Jayprakash%20Somani

Books are available online at International Market

4. Amazon International: https://www.amazon.com/s?k=jayprakash+somani

5. Amazon United Kingdom: https://www.amazon.co.uk/s?k=jayprakash+somani

6. E-Books/Kindle edition at National & International Level: https://www.amazon.in/s?k=jaypraksh+somani

82

Adv Jayprakash Somani's Online Courses

Download our app to get access to our Free Videos, Free Bare Acts, Free Study Material in Legal as well as International Business Regime.

Android App Link ;-https://clpandrea.page.link/cmSm

Ios APp Link :-https://apps.apple.com/us/app/classplus/id1324522260

Login with org code ;- (qywzji)

Web Link ;-https://qywzji.courses.store/

Download App on Google play store - Type

<u>Jayprakash Somani SupremeCourt</u>

Legal Courses :

1. SLP- Bail Matters- Drafting & Successful Arguing in the Supreme Court.

Description - This Course is helpful to Advocates, Litigants, Law Officers, Law Students, Law Schools, Individual. Course contains 8 Videos + Study Material+ PDF Books. Access to this course is for Two Years. Expected duration of this course is one month only.

Topics : 1. SLP- Bail Matters- Drafting & Successful Arguing in the Supreme Court, **2.** Types of bails, **3.** Laws related to bail matters, **4.** How to read Impugned Order of High Court & frame substantial question of laws, **5.** How to draft excellent SLP, **6.** Searching of citations/ case laws, **7.** How to argue in admission hearings, **8.** How argue in after notice hearing.

Speaker: Jayprakash Bansilal Somani, MBA (Foreign Trade), LL. B. Advocate, Supreme Court of India & IP www.jayprakashsomani.com Call: P. A. 9322188701

2. SLP- Succession Matters- Drafting & Successful Arguing in the Supreme Court.

Description - This Course is helpful to Advocates, Litigants, Law Officers, Law Students, Law Schools, Individual. Course contains 9 Videos + Study Material+ PDF Books. Access to this course is for Two Years. Expected duration of this course is one month only.

Topics :1. SLP- Succession Matters- Drafting & Successful Arguing in the Supreme Court, **2.** Information about Succession Matters, **3.** Laws related to Succession Matters, **4.** How to read Impugned Order of High Court to frame substantial questions of law, **5.** How to draft excellent synopsis & list of date, **6.** Drafting of SLP of Succession Matter, **7.** Searching of citations/ case laws, **8.** How to prepare notes & then argue in admission hearings, **9.** How to prepare notes & then argue in after notice final hearing.

Speaker: Jayprakash Bansilal Somani, MBA (Foreign Trade), LL. B. Advocate, Supreme Court of India & IP www.jayprakashsomani.com Call: P. A. 9322188701

3. Legal Vocabulary & its practice pattern to Argue in High Court and Supreme Court / Improve Your Legal English

Description - This Course is helpful to Advocates, Litigants, Law Officers, Law Students, Law Schools, Individual. Course contains 11 Videos + Study Material+ PDF Books. Access to this course is for Two Years. Expected duration of this course is three month only.

Topics : **1.** Legal Vocabulary & its practice pattern to Argue in High Court and Supreme Court / Improve Your Legal English, **2.** 1000 legal verbs with its three forms, **3.** Twelve Tenses with its running practice, **4.** One Pdf book on legal vocabulary & its practice pattern with Latin Terms, **5.** Second Pdf book on legal vocabulary & its practice pattern with Latin Terms, **6.** Some Videos of CJI Dr. Dhananjay Chandrachud for the practice of good legal English, **7.** Some Video/Audio Lectures of Legend Nani Palkhivala for standard perfect legal English & flow of Speech, **8.** Some Videos of renowned Sr. Advocates from Mumbai for flow, legal vocabulary & their struggle in legal journey, **9.** Some Videos of Sr. Advocates of the Supreme Court for flow & legal vocabulary, **10.** Some Videos of foreign persons to improve Professional English & thinking process in English, **11.** Some important legal doctrines with case laws.

Speaker: Jayprakash Bansilal Somani, MBA (Foreign Trade), LL. B. Advocate, Supreme Court of India & IP www.jayprakashsomani.com Call: P. A. 9322188701.

4. SLP- Property Matters - Drafting and Successful Arguing in the Supreme Court.

Description - This Course is helpful to Advocates, Litigants, Law Officers, Law Students, Law Schools 8 Individual. Course contains 9 Videos + Study Material+ PDF Books. Access to this course is for Two Years. Expected duration of this course is one month only.

Topics : 1. SLP- Property Matters - Drafting and Successful Arguing in the Supreme Court, **2.** Types of Property Matters, **3.** Laws related to Property Matters, **4.** How to read Impugned Order of High Court to guide client & frame substantial question of laws, **5.** How to draft Synopsis & List of Dates in Property Matter, **6.** How to draft excellent SLP of Property Matter, **7.** Searching of citations/ case laws with specific paras, **8.** How to argue confidently in admission hearings, **9.** How argue confidently in after notice & final hearings.

Speaker: Jayprakash Bansilal Somani, MBA (Foreign Trade), LL. B. Advocate, Supreme Court of India & IP www.jayprakashsomani.com Call: P. A. 9322188701.

International Business Courses -

1. Agri Products Exports - Scope from India.

Description - This Course is helpful to Agriculturalists, Entrepreneurs, Exporters, Importers, Students. Course contains 12 Videos + Study Material+ PDF Books. Access to this course is for Two Years. Expected duration of this course is one month only.

Topics : 1- Agri Products Exports - Scope from India, **2.** Agri Export's share in India's total export, **3.** Agri Export Promotional Council's Support, **4.** Top 10 Agri export countries, **5.** Top 10 Agri export product, **6.** India's share in World's Agri Exports, **7.** Onion Exports from India, **8.** Rice Exports from India, **9.** Mango Exports from India, **10.** Fresh Vegetable Exports, **11.** Fresh Fruits Exports, **12.** Export of Agri Allied Products.

Speaker: Jayprakash Bansilal Somani, MBA (Foreign Trade), LL. B. Advocate, Supreme Court of India & IP www.jayprakashsomani.com Call: P. A. 9322188701.

2. Textile Exports - Scope from India.

Description - This Course is helpful to Textile Business Houses, Entrepreneurs, Exporters, Importers, Students. Course contains 14 Videos

+ Study Material+ PDF Books. Access to this course is for Two Years. Expected duration of this course is one month only.

Topics : **1**- Textile Exports - Scope from India, **2**. Textile Export's share in India's total exports, **3**. Support of Textile Export Promotional Council, **4**. Top 10 Countries in Textile Exports, **5**. Top 10 Products in Textile Exports, **6**. Export of Readymade Garments, **7**. Export of Man-made Textiles, **8**. Export of Handloom Products, **9**. Export of Wool & Woollen Textiles, **10**. Export of Silk, **11**. Exports of Handicrafts & Carpets, **12**. Exports of Coir & Coir Manufacturers, **13**. Exports of Jute,14. India's share in World's total textile expor.

Speaker: Jayprakash Bansilal Somani, MBA (Foreign Trade), LL. B. Advocate, Supreme Court of India & IP www.jayprakashsomani.com Call: P. A. 9322188701.

3. Export Import Procedure -Perfect Documentation & It's Management.

Description -This Course is helpful to Business Men, Service Providers, Entrepreneurs, Exporters, Importers, Students. Course contains 13 Videos + Study Material+ PDF Books. Access to this course is for Two Years. Expected duration of this course is three months only.

Topics : **1**. Export Import Procedure, Perfect Documentation & Its management, **2**. Company Formation, **3**. Opening of Bank Account in AD Bank, **4**. Export Procedure points, **5**. Import Procedure Points, **6**. Taking Import Export Code, **7**. Taking RCMC number, **8**. Registration at Port when necessary, **9**. Quality Inspection Certificate of Goods, **10**. CHA & its roll, **11**. Custom Formalities, **12**. Export Documents such as Invoice, Bill of Lading, Insurance Certificate, Quality Inspection Certificate & others, **13**. Excellent Management of Export & Imports Documents.

Speaker: Jayprakash Bansilal Somani, MBA (Foreign Trade), LL. B. Advocate, Supreme Court of India & IP www.jayprakashsomani.com Call: P. A. 9322188701.

4. Jewellery Exports -Scope from India

Description - You can understand world wide scope for Jems & Jewellery in multidimensional ways. 14 videos of this course will create positive spark among you to enter into the Exports & Imports of Gems & Jewellery and other products. Chance to ask your query to Somani Sir every week.

Topics :**1**. Jewellery Exports - Scope from India, **2**. Jewellery Export's share in India's total exports, **3**. Support of Jems & Jewellery Export

Promotional Council, **4.** Top 10 Countries in Jewellery Exports, **5.** Top 10 Products in Jewellery Exports, **6.** Export of Cut & Polished Diamonds, **7.** Export of Gold Jewellery, **8.** Export of Plain Gold Jewellery, **9.** Export of Studded Gold Jewellery, **10.** Export of Silver Jewellery, **11.** Exports of Platinum Jewellery, **12.** Exports of Imitation Jewellery, **13.** Exports of Articles of Gold, Silver & others, **14.** India's share in World's total Jewellery export.

Speaker: Jayprakash Bansilal Somani, MBA (Foreign Trade), LL. B. Advocate, Supreme Court of India & IP www.jayprakashsomani.com Call: P. A. 9322188701.

5. Export Import Finance Management with LC, ECGC & Venture Capital.

Description -You can understand A to Z about International Finance with LC, ECGC & Venture Capital in simple language & with illustrations. 11 videos of this course will create positive spark among you regarding International Finance Management with practical tips. Chance to ask your query to Somani Sir every week.

Topics : 1. Export Import Finance Management with LC, ECGC & Venture Capital, **2.** Which is good & excellent source of finance, **3.** Banking Finance, **4.** List of Banks which provides finance for International Business, **5.** How to start business in Less or Zero Capital, **6.** Letter of Credit, **7.** Types of LCs **8.** Scrutiny of L/C, **9.** ECGC Policy, **10.** Venture Capital Finance., **11.** Ideal formula of Investment & continues growth.

Speaker: Jayprakash Bansilal Somani, MBA (Foreign Trade), LL. B. Advocate, Supreme Court of India & IP www.jayprakashsomani.com Call: P. A. 9322188701.

6. Shipping & Logistics in International Business with live links of Ports, ICDs, CHAs etc.

Description - This Course is helpful to any Businessman, Professionals, Entrepreneurs, Exporters, Importers, CHAs, & Students.

Course contains following 10 Videos + Study Material+ PDF Books. Access to this course is for Two Years. Expected duration of this course is three months only.

Topics : 1. Shipping & Logistics in International Business with live links of Ports, ICDs, CHAs etc, **2.** Roll of CHA in Shipping & Logistics of International Business, **3.** How to find good & genuine CHA, **4.** Courier/ post service for small parcel, **5.** India's important Ports & ICDs with live links, **6.** How & what to study Ports/ ICDs websites, **7.** Art to reduce charges of Shipping & logistics, **8**. Information about some Top International Ports with live links, **9**. Roll of Customs in Exports & Imports,**10**. How to become CHA .

Speaker: Jayprakash Bansilal Somani, MBA (Foreign Trade), LL. B. Advocate, Supreme Court of India & IP www.jayprakashsomani.com Call: P. A. 9322188701.

7. International Business Marketing Part 1: Finding Potential & Genuine Buyers for Exports and Suppliers for Imports.

Description -You can understand Seven Excellent ways to Find Potential & Genuine Buyers for Exports and Suppliers for Imports with illustrations. 11 videos of this course will create positive spark among you regarding International Business Marketing with practical tips. Chance to ask your query to Somani Sir every week.

Topics : 1. International Business Marketing Part 1: Finding Potential & Genuine Buyers for Exports and Suppliers for Imports,**2**. Seven Excellent Ways to find Potential Buyers for Exports, **3**. Top 20 B to B Websites in the World, **4**. Searching Potential Buyers from B to B Sites. Is this safe & good way to search potential buyers, **5**. Searching Potential Buyers through Export Promotional Councils & Its Magazines, **6**. Searching Potential Buyers with help from Embassies, **7**. Searching Potential Buyers through Chamber of Commerce at global level, **8**. Searching Potential Buyers from International Trade Fairs & Exhibitions, **9**. Searching Potential Buyers through your friends & relatives or any Indian Person in focus countries, **10**. How to find focus countries for your products or services, **11**. Taking references from establish buyer/seller.

Speaker: Jayprakash Bansilal Somani, MBA (Foreign Trade), LL. B. Advocate, Supreme Court of India & IP www.jayprakashsomani.com Call: P. A. 9322188701.

8. International Business Marketing Part 2: Communication Skill to take repeated orders from Potential Buyers

Description - You can learn Perfect Communication Skills to initiate International Trade with foreign buyers and art to take repeated orders from these Potential Buyers with illustrations. 11 videos of this course will create positive spark among you to reach upto One Star Exporter Level rapidly and subsequent journey to reach upto Five Star Export House. Chance to ask your query to Somani Sir every week.

Topics :1. International Business Marketing Part 2: Communication Skill to take repeated orders from Potential Buyers,**2**. Preparation of

Impressive Company Profile, **3.** Excellent Product CatLog for International Market, **4.** Phone Calls with maintaining dignity of ourself & our country, **5.** Sending emails, **6.** Sending what's app messages, **7.** Technique of repeated follow up, **8.** Art of taking 100% advance payments, **9.** Before giving credit facility how to look credibility of potential buyers or suppliers, **10.** Art of earning good profit of margin, **11.** Art of managing international clients.

Speaker: Jayprakash Bansilal Somani, MBA (Foreign Trade), LL. B. Advocate, Supreme Court of India & IP www.jayprakashsomani.com Call: P. A. 9322188701.